The Corridors of Time · IV ·

PRIESTS & KINGS

By HAROLD PEAKE and
HERBERT JOHN FLEURE

OXFORD: AT THE CLARENDON PRESS

1927

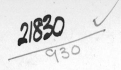

PREFACE

WHEN cultivation leads to permanent settlement and this, again, to intercourse and trade, villages may grow into cities and written records may be kept; kings and priests then become prominent features of civilization.

The present volume sketches this phase of evolution, and the authors have ventured to use the reckoning of the earliest records, with a few adjustments that have been explained. The dates given must, however, be considered quite tentative, however exact they may appear, for the authors have felt it unwise to reduce them to 'round figures'.

The rise of kings and priests in the old riverine lands is followed by great spreads into Europe and Asia of peasants and traders; the descriptions of these movements make use of much recently published work. These descriptions are supplemented by a short sketch of the drifts of mankind and of his racial types, because these later but supremely important drifts seem to be linked up with the great spreads of civilization here described.

Many thanks are due to the authors, editors, and publishers of the following works and journals for permission to reproduce figures: *Mémoires de la Société Royale des Antiquaires du Nord*, 1908–9 (Gyldendalske Boghandel Nordisk Forlag, Copenhagen), for fig. 1 (right); *Vorgeschichte Nordamerikas*, 1894, by E. Schmidt (Friedr. Vieweg & Sohn, Brunswick), for fig. 2; *The Royal Tombs of the Earliest Dynasties*, Part II, by W. M. Flinders Petrie (Egypt Exploration Society), for figs. 4 and 34; *Beni Hasan*, Part I, by P. Newberry (Egypt Exploration Society), for fig. 40; *The Babylonian Expedition of the University of Pennsylvania: Series A: Cuneiform Texts*, vol. xx, part I, by H. V. Hilprecht (Dept. of Archaeology, University of Pennsylvania), for fig. 5; *Vasiliki*, by R. Seagar (The Museum of the University of Pennsylvania), for fig. 57; *Annual of the British School at Athens*, vol. vii, for fig. 65; vol. x, for figs. 58, 59, and 66; and vol. xxii, for figs. 73 and 74; *A History of Egypt*, 2nd edition, by J. H. Breasted (Scribner's Sons, U.S.A.; Hodder & Stoughton, Ltd., England), for figs. 11, 46, 47, 53, and 54; *A History of Sumer and Akkad*, by L. W. King (Chatto & Windus), for figs. 15, 22, and 26; *Report on the Excavation of the 'A' Cemetery at Kish, Mesopotamia*, Part I, by E. MacKay (Field Museum of Natural History, Chicago), for fig. 16; *Corpus Vasorum Antiquorum*, Paris, Louvre, Fasc. 2 (Oxford University Press), for fig. 17; *Découvertes en Chaldée*, by E. de Sarzec (Librairie Ernest Leroux, Paris), for fig. 19; *Nouvelles fouilles de Tello*, by G. Cros, L. Heuzey, and F. Thureau-Dangin (Librairie Ernest Leroux), for fig. 23; *Chaldea*, by Z. A. Ragozin (Benn, Ltd.), for fig. 24; *The Dawn of Mediterranean Civilization*, by A. Mosso (Benn, Ltd.), for fig. 56; *From Tribe to Empire*, by A. Moret (La Renaissance du Livre, Paris), for fig. 28; *Studies in Early Pottery of the Near East*, Part I, by H. Frankfort (Royal Anthropological Institute), for fig. 30; Veröff. der Ernst von Sieglin Expedition in Agypten, vol. i: *Das Grabdenkmal des Königs Chephren*, by U. Hölscher, L. Borchardt and G. Steindorff (Verlag J. C. Hinrich'sche Buchhandlung, Leipzig), for fig. 38; *The Ancient Egyptians and their Influence upon the Civilization of Europe*, by G. Elliot Smith (Harper & Brothers), for fig. 42; *Ancient Times*, by J. H. Breasted (Ginn & Co., Ltd.), for figs. 43 and 48; *Tombs of the Third Egyptian Dynasty at Reqaqnah and Bet Khallaf*, by J. Garstang (Constable & Co., Ltd.), for fig. 44; *History of Art in Ancient Egypt*, vol. ii, by G. Perrot and Ch. Chipiez (Chapman & Hall, Ltd.), for fig. 45; *A History of Egypt*, by W. M. Flinders Petrie (Methuen & Co., Ltd.), for fig. 49; *Unpublished Objects from Palaikastro*, 1923, Supplementary Paper I (British School at Athens), for fig. 55; *The Vaulted Tombs of Mesara*, by S. Xanthoudides (University Press of Liverpool, Ltd.), for figs. 62 and 64; *Prehistoric Aegean Pottery*, by E. J. Forsdyke (British Museum) for fig. 69; *Prehistoric Thessaly*, by A. J. B. Wace and M. S. Thompson (Cambridge University Press), for figs. 75–8 and 80; *Scythians and Greeks*, by E. H. Minns (Cambridge University Press), for fig. 103; *Ilios*, by H. Schliemann (John Murray), for figs. 81 and 92; *Troja*, by H. Schliemann (John Murray), for fig. 82; *Explorations in Turkestan*, vol. i, by R. Pumpelly, W. M. Davis, R. W. Pumpelly, and E. Huntingdon (Carnegie Institution of Washington), for figs. 83–6; *Wiener Praehistorische Zeitschrift*, vol. i, for fig. 93; *Berlin Praehistorische Zeitschrift*, vol. ii, for fig. 91; *Zeitschrift für Ethnologie*, 1911 (Julius Springer, Berlin), for fig. 100.

We wish also to thank the Kyrle Enlarging Company of Stanford Dingley for permission to reproduce the photographs forming figure 62 in Peasants and Potters.

H. J. E. P.

H. J. F.

October 1927.

CONTENTS

1. The Discovery of Metal . . 7
2. Systems of Chronology . . 16
3. Sumer and Akkad . . . 38
4. The Old Kingdom of Egypt . 61
5. Early Minoan Times . . 97
6. The Aegean World . . 112
7. The North Kurgan at Anau . 133
8. The Peasants of the Danube Basin 138
9. The Valley of the Alt . . 153
10. The Black Earth Lands . . 161
11. Chronological Summary . . 170
12. The Races of the World . . 181

LIST OF ILLUSTRATIONS

1. Stone dagger with metal prototype . . . 9
2. Axe of hammered copper 10
3. Map showing the distribution of copper ores in the Near East . 13
4. Portions of sard and gold sceptre of Khasekhemui . . 15
5. One of the Nippur tablets 18
6. Astrological tablet. By the courtesy of the British Museum . 21
7. Tablet of the eighth century B.C., from Kish, copied from a lost original of the time of Ammizaduga (twentieth century). Ashmolean Museum, Oxford . . . 23
8. Chronological Chart of Mesopotamian dynasties . . 27
9. The Nile in flood. From a photograph kindly lent by Sir Henry Lyons 29
10. Portion of the Kahun papyrus describing the heliacal rising of Sothis. Reproduced by the courtesy of Das Staatliche Museum, Berlin 31
11. The Palermo Stele 33
12. Chart of the early dynasties of Egypt . . . 35
13. Chart of Minoan Periods 37
14. Map of the Mesopotamia Plain 39
15. Mace-head of Mesilim 40
16. Pottery from Cemetery A at Kish. From a photograph kindly lent by the Field Museum of Natural History, Chicago . . 41
17. Pottery from Susa II 43
18. Limestone figure of a king of Maer in the British Museum. Photograph by Mansell 45
19. Plaque representing Ur-Nina, king of Lagash, and his family . 47
20. Portion of the Stele of the Vultures. Photograph by Giraudon . 48
21. Silver vase dedicated to Ningirsu by Entemena. Photograph by Alinari 51
22. Impression of a seal of Lugal-anda . . . 52
23. Tombs at Lagash 53
24. Cylinder said to be of Sargon of Agade . . . 55

25. Map of the Dominions of Sargon of Agade . . . 57
26. Alabaster statue of Manishtissu, dedicated by a high official to the god Naruti 58
27. Stele of Naram-Sin, king of Agade, representing the king and his allies in triumph over their enemies. Photograph by Giraudon . 59
28. The red crown of Lower Egypt and the white crown of Middle Egypt 62
29. Map of Egypt 65
30. Boat and bird with fish on an Egyptian vase . . . 66
31. Boat and bowl with fish on a vase from Lagash, in the Louvre. Photograph by M. Desboutin 67
32. Mace-head of 'the Scorpion'. Ashmolean Museum, Oxford . 68
33. Slate palette of Narmer. British Museum . . . 71
34. Tomb of Khasekhemui, at Abydos 72
35. The pyramid of Zoser, at Sakkara. Photograph by Mr. Percival Hart 73
36. Pyramid attributed to Snefru at Medûm. Photograph by Exclusive News Agency 74
37. The Great Pyramid of Khufu at Giza. Photograph by Bonfils . 75
38. Restoration of the pyramids of Abusir and connecting buildings. After Borchardt 77
39. Life-size statue of the son of Pepi I. Cairo Museum . . 78
40. A noble of the Old Kingdom hunting wild fowl . . . 79
41. Chart of the Kings of the Old Kingdom of Egypt . . . 81
42. Profile of a skull from the Giza necropolis showing Armenoid traits 83
43. Diagram showing the evolution of the Egyptian tomb from the sand-heap to the pyramid 85
44. Third dynasty arch, from a tomb at Bet Khallaf . . . 86
45. Villa and garden of an Egyptian noble of the Old Kingdom. After Perrot and Chipiez 87
46. Workmen drilling out stone vessels 88
47. Metalworkers' workshop in the Old Kingdom . . . 89
48. Representation of a sea-going ship, found among the wall reliefs in the pyramid temple of Sahure 90
49. Granite statue No. 1, Memphis 91
50. Wooden statue of the Sheikh el-Beled. Photograph by Underwood Press Service 92
51. Body of a woman from a predynastic burial in Egypt. Reproduced, by kind permission, from the collections in the Field Museum of Natural History, Chicago 93
52. Head of King Khafre. Cairo Museum 94
53. Elevation of part of the colonnade surrounding the court of the pyramid temple of Nuserre (fifth dynasty) . . . 95
54. The celestial barque of the sun-god, with other deities on board . 96
55. Clay model of a boat of the Second Early Minoan period . 98
56. Amulets, which are thought to represent mummies. *a*, from Egypt ; *b*, from Hagia Triada, Crete 100
57. Plan of Early Minoan II buildings at Vasiliki . . . 102
58. Pottery of the First Early Minoan Period 103
59. Grained chalices on a wooden model 104
60. Copper daggers from Crete 105
61. The treasure of Mochlos. Photograph by G. Maraghiannie, Candia 106
62. The tholos of Kalathiana 107
63. Diagrammatic plan and section of a tholos . . . 108
64. Modern cheese dairy on Mount Ida 109
65. The Great Mother and horns of consecration. From a sealing . 110
66. Vases from the cave at Miamu 111
67. Map of the Aegean World 113

68. Chart of the early civilizations of the Aegean region . . 115
69. Incised vase of Early Cycladic II 116
70. Silver diadem from the acropolis of Chalandriani in Syros . . 117
71. Cycladic tombs. 1, Syros ; 2, Euboea 118
72. Figure of the Great Mother. In private possession . . 119
73. Pottery of Early Helladic type 120
74. Early Helladic pot 121
75. Pot of Thessalian red ware from Tsangli 123
76. Pots from Tsangli 125
77. Painted pots of Thessalian I from Tsangli 127
78. Plan of House T at Tsangli 128
79. Thessalian celts. After Tsountas 129
80. Thessalian figurines. After Wace and Thompson . . 130
81. Troy as it appeared after the excavations of 1879 . . 131
82. Jugs from the first settlement at Hissarlik . . . 132
83. Pivotal door-stone of house 134
84. Pottery from Anau II 135
85. Pot from Anau II 136
86. Dagger blade from Anau II 137
87. Map of the Danube Basin 139
88. Shoe-last celts. After Seger 141
89. Spiral-meander ware 143
90. Carinated pots of stroke-ornamented ware . . . 144
91. Pedestalled bowls from Vinča 147
92. Face-urn from Hissarlik 148
93. Gourd-shaped vessels of the First Danubian period. After J. L. Pič 151
94. Map of the basin of the Alt 155
95. Clay stamp or pintadera 156
96. Painted cup from Erösd. After Laszlo 157
97. Pottery from the Alt valley 158
98. Actual potter's oven and model found at Erösd. After Laszlo . 159
99. Clay figurines from the Alt valley 160
100. Pottery from Cucuteni A 163
101. Clay figurines from Cucuteni A 164
102. Vases from Horodnica. B has been drawn, by permission, from a
    photograph kindly lent by Professor Dr. Josez-ul-Kostrzewski . 165
103. Pottery from Tripolye A 166
104. Map of The Black Earth Region 167
105. General Chronological Chart 173
106. Migrations of the Grain Growers 175
107. Statue of an Egyptian princess in the Turin Museum. Photograph
    by Anderson 179
108. The suggested ' cradle ' of modern man 183
109. Map of the East Indian Region as reconstructed . . . 185
110. The Plynlymon type. Photograph by Mr. L. H. Dudley Buxton,
    reproduced by his kind permission 187
111. An American Indian from the plains. Photograph by Mr. L. H.
    Dudley Buxton, reproduced by kind permission of the Editor
    from *Discovery*, 1925 190
112. An Asiatic Alpine from Turkestan. Reproduced, by kind permis-
    sion, from the collection of photographs presented to the Royal
    Geographical Society in 1878 by the Russian General Kaufmann 193
113. A Mongol 195
114. A Zulu girl. Photograph by Messrs. York & Son . . . 197
115. The Mediterranean type. Portrait of himself by Rafael in the
    Uffizi Gallery. Photograph, Rischgitz Collection . . 201

The Discovery of Metal

It was natural that the pioneers in the study of early history should have roughed out a scheme of successive ages of Stone, Bronze, and Iron ; and that, having gone thus far, they should soon have noted that some groups of stone implements showed chipping only, while others included specimens that were ground and often polished as well. Thus, they were led to the idea of the Palaeolithic and Neolithic Ages, both lying within the Stone Age and preceding the Age of Bronze. This old framework is showing signs of strain at many points as exploration progresses, and the transitions between these ages are appearing as important phases in themselves. Most of what was classed as Early Neolithic is now considered a Palaeolithic survival, while a great deal that was looked upon as Late Neolithic is now held to belong to the period when metal was first entering into use. It is known that the finely chipped flint arrow-head, long held to be Neolithic, was used by peoples in the early days of metal. It is also becoming increasingly probable that the axe of ground or polished stone spread from the centre which, at a not very different time, learned to use copper as well, though the spread of the axe of ground stone was more rapid and more general than that of metal. The axe of ground stone was often superior in practice to a copper axe, and its use continued in some places even after bronze was known near by.

The Neolithic Age is thus losing its distinctness. It must be remembered that, while some peoples were still in the Palaeolithic stage, others had advanced beyond it. The Neolithic Age is thus becoming a rather loose term applicable to certain regions, and covering a period when modified survivals of the Palaeolithic Age prevailed, together with ideas that filtered in from more advanced regions. These ideas originated in centres that included metal among their elements of culture, but spread more rapidly and to more distant regions than did the knowledge of metal. For the production of metal some organization is desirable, and we do not need to emphasize the idea that a caste of metallurgical craftsmen would not be likely to make its methods public.

There seems little doubt that gold was the first metal to attract interest; the attraction may have developed independently among many peoples at many places. Elliot Smith suggests a start by the finding of a small nugget to serve as a bead in place of an older-fashioned shell or stone in a necklace. We would recall the glittering grains in the sands of sunlit streams and would suggest that they might be collected, at first on the hand and later on a fleece placed in the water to catch the flakes borne down. Collecting the flakes and hammering them into little plates or leaves to be used as covers for various objects would be simple developments. The crushing of quartz veins for the extraction of gold is a later invention, more likely to have had a single origin than the earlier and simpler process.

However attractive gold might be, its softness and its rarity precluded at first the possibility of its working a revolution in everyday life. It was only when in the course of time its attractiveness and rarity combined to make it a standard of exchange that it acquired its enormous influence. From the first, however, it may well have tempted prospectors far afield.

It was otherwise with copper. This metal is hard enough to be used as material for certain tools, and these, by their fineness, made possible more delicate work than could well be executed with stone or bone. The hardness of ground stone axes,

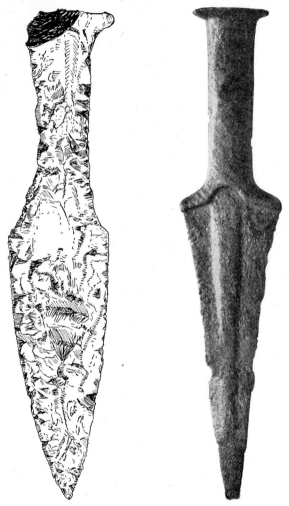

FIG. I. Stone dagger with metal prototype.

however, led to their retention for many purposes until the alloying of copper with tin to secure hard bronze was mastered. It was also possible to hammer out new shapes of tools in copper, to make casts, to perforate lumps and, generally, to open up endless new possibilities. It was thus the introduction of copper and especially of its harder alloys that made a revolution in civilization.

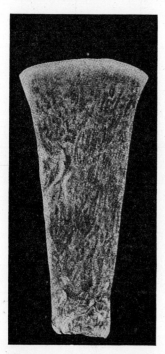

Elliot Smith imagines that copper was discovered by an early Egyptian, who threw into the fire a lump of malachite that proved too refractory to be ground upon his palette, and who subsequently discovered in the ashes a copper bead. This is but one of many possibilities. For a long time men had had reasons for putting stones into a fire, and no doubt already knew how to get an air-draught to brighten the fire's glow. They would naturally build their fires on a stone base rather than on wet earth, and in many regions, before cauldrons were known, they

Fig. 2. Axe of hammered copper.

heated stones red hot and poled them into a trough to warm the water for cooking. With stones thus put into fires it might well happen that a piece of native copper might be melted into beads which would be afterwards found in the ashes, or that malachite, or even copper pyrites, might be reduced to metallic form in the same way. These lumps of metal would attract attention if only by their brightness, and they would be found malleable ;　so men would experiment with stones until they learned the source of this new treasure.　Its discovery was thus an opportunity for the liberation of initiative in the direction of prospecting for the raw material, and this activity in turn seems to have been an important factor of the impetus to develop means of communication and transport.　These served to multiply contacts between peoples of different traditions, leading to the weakening of old habits and the invention of new schemes of work and life.

We would urge that the idea of a sharp distinction between the Neolithic and Bronze Ages is superannuated, and would picture a transition in several successive phases.　A knowledge of shiny malleable beads and even of the ores whence they could be obtained may surely have arisen more than once. The hammering of copper was undoubtedly the first means of shaping implements in that material, and this again may well have been adopted independently by different peoples; but, when the details of the copper implements of two regions are very similar, we picture a transmission of the art from the one to the other, or contacts leading to a joint development. We may note in passing that the shaping of copper implements by hammering already gave opportunities, unknown to workers in stone, of varying the shapes and the methods of hafting the implements ;　this led to a liberation of initiative beyond that already noted.　Tempering is another addition to the copper workers' art, and casting another and later stage ;　finally the art of alloying was added.　These refinements of early metallurgy are less likely than the initial processes to have arisen independently at more than one centre.

Alloying was not, however, established all at once.　Almost every source of copper contains other metals admixed even if only in small proportions, and among these accessories tin sometimes occurs. These impurities differ in the different copper ores, and it may be possible to trace the source of the material of copper and bronze implements by quantitative analyses. Up to the present very few of these have been made, but a Committee of the Anthropological Section of the British Association has taken up this interesting line of research. Though it is still too early to draw conclusions, there is a possibility that a very early source of copper may have been the deposits of native copper which still exist at Arghana, about seventy-five miles north-west of Diarbekr. Several other deposits, some of which are known to have been worked at an early date, occur in the neighbourhood of Diarbekr and Erzeroum, while others are being worked at the present time between Sinope and Trebizond. Thus, the discovery of copper may well have taken place somewhere in the upper basin of the Tigris and Euphrates, probably not far from the places at which they emerge from the hills on to the Fertile Crescent.

However this may be we cannot doubt that the establishment of the standard alloy, with 10 per cent. of tin, came only through many experiments and after frequent observation of the special hardness of the metal derived from ores that happened to include a fair proportion of tin. The establishment of such a standard, the invention of standard bronze, seems to us a step that is likely to have been made by one group of inventors only, and to have spread from one centre. Where that centre was it is still too early to argue, but indications are accumulating which seem to suggest that it may possibly have been in the Aegean or in Spain, though the Fertile Crescent cannot be entirely disregarded. Langdon has suggested that *Kuki* is an ancient form of the name ' Cyprus ', for *Ku* in his opinion is an ancient word for copper ; a number of other scholars, however,

believe that *Ku* stood for tin or possibly lead, and note that
there is another Sumerian word for copper.

If our argument has been followed it will be seen that we
are inclined to use as a hypothesis the idea of the spread from
a single centre of what may be called the complete art of bronze
making. We picture it spreading to regions some of which were

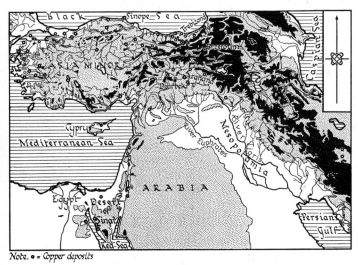

Note. ● = *Copper deposits*

FIG. 3. Map showing the distribution of copper ores in the Near East.

already acquainted with copper ; in some of these regions
the inhabitants already made implements from this metal, in
others, perhaps, beads only of this substance were used. The
knowledge of bronze may also have spread to regions in which
until then only wood, stone, and bone had been used, though
they may, in some cases, have felt the influence of other waves
of culture allied, as we believe, to that of metal working.
These would be waves which introduced the cultivation of

grain, the domestication of animals, the grinding and even the polishing of stone axes, and the fine flaking of barbed flint arrow-heads.

In the Eastern Mediterranean, Egypt, and the Fertile Crescent, a copper age preceded that of bronze, and the same fact seems established for the Danubian lands and, with less certainty, for Switzerland. The same is true for South Italy, Sicily, Spain, and Western France, and, so some think, for Ireland. In the last case some of the copper implements are by no means early in form. The island, too, was rich in copper, but apparently dependent on outside sources for tin. It seems likely, therefore, that the natives of Ireland made copies in copper of the implements made for them or brought to them by immigrants from lands where bronze was more easily produced. The possibility of an analogous interpretation of copper implements elsewhere, as in South Spain, should be borne in mind. In England and Scandinavia, on the other hand, we seem to have little indication of a copper age, and it is worth noting that it was the scholars in these lands who first established the classification of periods as Neolithic and Bronze Ages.

The method of tracing by quantitative analyses the sources of the copper used for implements has been applied in a remarkable fashion to the identification of one of the ancient sources of gold. It has been noticed, for example, that a fragment of gold, found in the tomb of King Khasekhemui of the third dynasty of Egypt, has a red antimoniate crust. Antimony combines with gold, so far as is known, only in the presence of tellurium, and the only region in the Old World in which gold and tellurium occur mixed is within the ring of the Carpathian mountains. The only rich gold-field within this ring is in Transylvania, where gold has been worked at least from

Roman times onwards. In the eastern part of Transylvania lies the valley of the Alt, and the precious metal is still found near this basin, while there is a copper-mine close to the source of the river. At various places in this valley have been found important early settlements, the inhabitants of which knew both gold and copper. Another early settlement, with a different culture, has been found at Tordos, in the Maros valley, in the very heart of the gold region. We must leave a fuller description of these settlements to a later chapter, though it

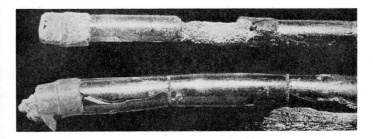

FIG. 4. Portions of sard and gold sceptre of Khasekhemui.

will not be possible to make this as full as we could wish until an important manuscript, giving a full account of the excavation of some of these sites, has been published. Meanwhile, we note the possibility that gold from Transylvania found its way to Egypt about 3,000 B.C.

Of the early use of silver we know little. It does not seem to have come into general use much before the discovery of bronze. From the little that we know at present we may suspect that it was first found and used in Asia Minor, probably in the west of that province, though it is found more abundantly in the eastern mountains, where, as we have seen, copper ores are not uncommon.

Systems of Chronology

IF we wish to reconstruct the history of a period, still more the whole history of human times, it is important that we should know as accurately as possible the order in which events occurred, or in which periods they should be placed. That is to say we must have a system of chronology. If we are uncertain of the lengths of our periods or of the time that elapsed between successive events, and know only their general sequence, we have to be content with what is known as a Relative Chronology ; if, on the other hand, we can measure these periods and intervals by years, and if, moreover, we can carry our measurements back from the present day, we have established a Positive Chronology.

During those far-distant epochs, before man appeared upon the scene, which we know as Geological Times, we have to be content with a relative chronology, for such estimates of time as have been made vary very widely. Even during the Ice Age our position is little better, and until after the maximum of the last or Würm glaciation we have nothing of value as a guide to the duration of time and we have avoided adding to the ' hecatomb of erroneous dates ' deplored by Baron de Geer.

After the passing of the first maximum of the Würm, and still more after the second maximum had gone by, we have, thanks to the Swedish geologists, the basis of a positive chronology. Though the figures we have given in our second part are not quite final, for de Geer has not completed his calculations, we are assured by him that the error is not likely to be large. The figures seemed sufficiently small and accurate to enable us to give them in terms of the Christian Era, though we have not felt justified in giving dates in lesser denominations than 500 years, and have realized that the margin of error is quite as large and conceivably larger than this figure.

For the Mesolithic Age in Europe we have been dependent, too, on similar geological evidence, and we have utilized this, also, in the last part when dealing with the early civilizations in the Near East. In that region, however, we have nearly reached the date of the first written documents, which enable us to form a positive chronology, in fact we have dealt with an inscription of a monarch whose dates can be estimated with fair precision. It has thus been possible to calculate backwards and so to arrive at a more detailed chronology. We have, therefore, ventured to suggest some dates in much smaller denominations.

In this part we shall be dealing with a period about which we have a vast number of contemporary written documents, and an almost continuous series of monarchs in Egypt and Mesopotamia, the lengths of whose reigns are in most cases known with fair precision. We can, therefore, give dates in terms of our era to all events described, sometimes to the actual year, or with a margin of only a few years. There are, however, certain details in this chronology on which experts differ, and these divergences in the case of Egypt are very wide. It becomes necessary, therefore, to describe the various systems in vogue, with the arguments advanced for and against each, and to give reasons for adopting those which are followed in these volumes.

Among the baked clay tablets covered with cuneiform inscriptions, which have been found in Mesopotamia, are some giving lists of kings of Babylonia and Assyria, and some giving synchronous lists of both; from these it has been possible to compile a complete chronology back almost to 1000 B.C. Early

in the Christian Era certain ecclesiastical writers, among them
Julius Africanus in the third century and Eusebius a little later,
attempted to draw up World Histories on a chronological basis.
These derived much of their information from Berosus, a priest
of the god Bel at Babylon, who had written a history of Chaldaea

FIG. 5.   One of the Nippur tablets.

between 280 and 261 B.C.   From these sources it has been
gathered that several successive dynasties ruled at Babylon, the
first of which was founded before 2000 B.C.   The numerous
cuneiform tablets that have been found give references to most
of these kings, and it has been possible to compile complete lists
of the monarchs of all these dynasties but the third, in which

the names of several of the kings are missing. In the vast majority of the remainder the lengths of their reigns are also known.

Had we a complete list of all these kings with the lengths of their reigns it might be possible to calculate the date of the foundation of the first dynasty, except that some slight errors would occur if the year in which a monarch ascended the throne were credited both to him and to his predecessor. Moreover, some of the dynasties might have been partly or wholly contemporary. Both these factors of error actually exist, for the second dynasty, which ruled only the area near the Persian Gulf, seems to have overlapped by some centuries the preceding dynasty.

Owing to these causes, and especially to the gap in the list of the third dynasty, it has been impossible to reconstruct a chronology by the method of dead reckoning, and there have been considerable differences between the computations of various scholars. Luckily we have now some means of settling the question on an astronomical basis, though there is still some difference of opinion as to how to interpret the evidence.

A tablet has long been known which describes the movements of the planet Venus during the reign of Ammizaduga, the tenth king of the first dynasty of Babylon, and later a partial duplicate of this was found. From these Father Kugler, S.J., a well-known Dutch astronomer, made various calculations. Of the many entries, he found that for his purpose the best was that which mentioned an occultation of the planet for three days beginning on the 28th day of Arahsamnu, the eighth month, in the sixth year of Ammizaduga. This occultation he attributed to the occurrence of a new moon, and he came to the conclusion that the observation must refer to 2036/5, 1972/1, or 1852/1 B.C. There were grave objections on other

grounds to the first and last of these years, so Kugler determined the sixth year of Ammizaduga as 1972/1 B.C.

This date determined by Kugler did not fit very well with
the chronology constructed by Weidner and accepted by many
German Assyriologists. He therefore looked into the matter
again, and in 1922 published an amended opinion giving the
date in question as 1796 B.C., which brought him into close
agreement with Weidner's system. Later on (in 1925) a fresh
fragment was found (see Fig. 7) which supplied the lines missing
from the top of the British Museum tablets shown in Fig. 6.
This fragment, now in the Ashmolean Museum, Oxford, has
enabled Fotheringham to confirm his calculations announced
late in 1923 that the date 1796/5 B.C. was impossible, and that
1916/5 B.C. was the only possible date for the sixth year of
Ammizaduga. This is the latest view that has been expressed
on this important subject, and, though it has not yet met
with universal acceptance, its accuracy has not been seriously
questioned. Though the solution may not be final, we believe
it wisest to accept it for the present.

The acceptance of Fotheringham's date means that the
foundation of the first dynasty of Babylon took place in 2169
B.C. From this we can calculate that Sin-muballit, the fifth
king of the dynasty, began his reign in 2087 B.C., and we know
that the Sumerian dynasty of Isin came to an end in the
twelfth year of Sin-muballit, that is to say in 2076 B.C.

Some years ago Professor Arno Poebel published a large but
imperfect cuneiform tablet from Nippur belonging to the
Museum of the University of Philadelphia, and later Dr. Leon
Legrain added a large fragment to it. This appeared to be a
list of kings, but it was too imperfect for its meaning to be clear.
Later still Mr. C. J. Weld-Blundell gave to the Ashmolean
Museum at Oxford a number of tablets, among which was a

Fɪɢ. 6. Astrological tablet. By the courtesy
of the British Museum.

fine clay prism, known as the Weld-Blundell prism or W-B 444. This prism contains a complete list of kings from the Flood to the end of the dynasty of Isin ; it mentions also eight ante-diluvian monarchs.   In another tablet, W-B 62, ten kings are given as reigning before the Deluge.   The Weld-Blundell prism is perfect except for a few small abrasions, and the faults in the text caused by these can, in some cases, be made good by refer-ence to the Nippur tablets.   It was composed in or soon after 2076 B.C., while the Nippur tablets are about forty-two years older.

It is not easy to determine what value we are to place on documents of this kind, documents about 4,000 years old, which profess to give a complete list of the kings reigning in Mesopo-tamia during the previous 3,000 years, with the length of each reign.   Langdon has accepted at its face value the whole of the document except the first few dynasties, while Hall and others would reduce the dates considerably, especially those prior to 3000 B.C., as they wish to allow for possible overlapping. We know that writing was used as early as the first dynasty of Ur, the third after the Flood, and we have an inscription of a king A-an-ni-pad-da, who says he was the son of Mes-an-ni-pad-da, king of Ur ; Mes-an-ni-pad-da's name figures in our list as the first king of the first dynasty of Ur.   It is clear from the well-developed form of the writing in this inscription, as well as from the more primitive type shown by some stray and undatable tablets that have been found, that the art of writing had been known for a long time, perhaps since the first dynasty of Kish, the first after the Flood.   Moreover, though Mes-an-ni-pad-da's name is the first of which a contemporary document has been found, the names of several of the other kings in the list have long been known from other sources.

On the whole we feel prepared to accept the list provisionally with a few adjustments. At one period there appear to be indications of an overlap, and in the earlier dynasties the reigns attributed to the kings are often of impossible length.

FIG. 7. Tablet of the 8th century B.C., from Kish, copied from a lost original of the time of Ammizaduga (20th century), Ashmolean Museum, Oxford.

On these grounds the antediluvian kings and the two first post-diluvian dynasties have been relegated to the realms of mythology. We prefer to treat them as legendary, to consider the lists approximately accurate as far as the numbers of the

kings are concerned, and to substitute estimated averages for
the preposterous lengths given for their reigns.

Following these principles we shall accept at their face
value the last eight dynasties, the tenth to the seventeenth
after the Flood. This will make the fourth dynasty of Kish
begin 2875 B.C. Before this are two dynasties, the third of
Kish and that of Akshak. Kug-Bau, the sole monarch of the
third dynasty of Kish, is thought to have reigned contem-
poraneously with some of the kings of Aksak, and the last king
of the latter dynasty, Gimil, has the same name as the first
king of the fourth dynasty of Kish. We are inclined to treat
them as the same and to consider that the seven years attributed to Gimil as king of Aksak are included in the twenty-five
years allotted to him as king of Kish. With these emendations
the dynasty of Akshak would have begun in 2961 B.C.

The three preceding dynasties, the second of Ur and those
of Adab and Maer, we are taking at their face value, so that the
first of these began 3295 B.C.; but the three preceding these,
the dynasties of Awan, the second of Kish and that of Hamasi,
all show some kings with reigns of improbable length. We find
that in the case of short dynasties the average length of a
reign is about twenty-five years, and we have adopted this
figure in these cases. This brings the first year of the dynasty
of Awan to 3575 B.C.

Before this was the first dynasty of Ur to which allusion
has already been made. The reigns of the kings of this dynasty
were all of normal length except the first, that of Mes-an-ni-
pad-da, to whom reference has already been made. His reign
of eighty years is too long for that of the founder of a dynasty,
but, since he was succeeded on the throne by his son A-an-ni-
pad-da, whose name does not appear in the list, the eighty years
is not too long for their combined reigns. We are, therefore,

prepared to accept the figures of the list for this dynasty, which places the foundation of the first dynasty of Ur at 3752 B.C.

Before this were two dynasties, the first of Kish and the first of Erech. In both these cases the lengths of the reigns attributed to their kings were many thousands of years. The figures are clearly valueless, but we do not for this reason feel disposed to discard the lists. At Erech there were twelve kings, and, as we find later eleven kings of Agade reigning for 181 years, we propose to allot about 200 years to this dynasty, and to consider its foundation as dating from about 3950 B.C. The same remarks apply also to the first dynasty of Kish, with its twenty-three kings. We have estimated the duration of this dynasty roughly at 300 years, which will bring its foundation to the close of the Flood period, which we have ventured to correlate with the Gschnitz glaciation in the Alps, or to 4250 B.C. We are inclined to allow about 400 years for the interval when the Mesopotamian plain was flooded and another 250 years for the eight or ten kings of various cities who reigned there before the Flood. This would bring the beginning of the list, when settlements first were made by the banks of the rivers, to about 4900 B.C.

The chronology of Egypt is in a somewhat similar position. Julius Africanus and Eusebius have preserved for us lists of dynasties and kings compiled in Greek by Manetho, an Egyptian priest who flourished under Ptolemy Soter, who reigned over Egypt from 323 to 285 B.C. This list, like that of the Babylonian kings, suffers from lack of information as to the exact beginning and ending of the reigns, and the suspicion that both reigns and dynasties overlapped. Some checking has been possible from the comparison of Manetho's list with that given in the Turin Papyrus of Kings, which was composed during the nineteenth dynasty and frequently gives, in addition to the years, the odd months and days of the king's reign. It is often, however, difficult to identify the kings mentioned in this papyrus, and, as the document has been much garbled by copyists, it must be used with caution. More important is the famous Palermo Stele, which gives lists of the kings of the first five dynasties. Though fragmentary, it provides some idea of the lengths of some of the reigns.

Thus we see that we cannot place too much reliance on the list of Manetho or that given in the Turin papyrus, but a very large number of inscriptions is known, and from these it has been possible to ascertain the lengths of the reigns of many kings, and, in a number of cases, to measure the overlap which occurred when a king admitted his heir to a co-regency with himself. From these data it would have been possible to calculate back to Menes, the founder of the first dynasty, by the method of dead reckoning, had it not been for two periods, known as the first and second intermediate periods, when there is an almost complete absence of data for our purpose.

The second of these intermediate periods is that in which Egypt was dominated by foreign rulers, known as the Hyksos or Shepherd Kings. Manetho credits them with a rule of 510 years, and does not appreciate the fact that one of the dynasties, which he places separately, was endeavouring to govern a section of the country during part of the period of Hyksos rule. Manetho's dates in this case are clearly unreliable. A similar period, with foreign invaders ruling in the north and native dynasties governing the south, occurs between the sixth and eleventh dynasties, and these two gaps prevent any accurate estimate being made of the whole period by means of dead reckoning.

As in the case of Mesopotamia, Egyptologists long looked for some astronomical evidence, and for long they looked in vain.

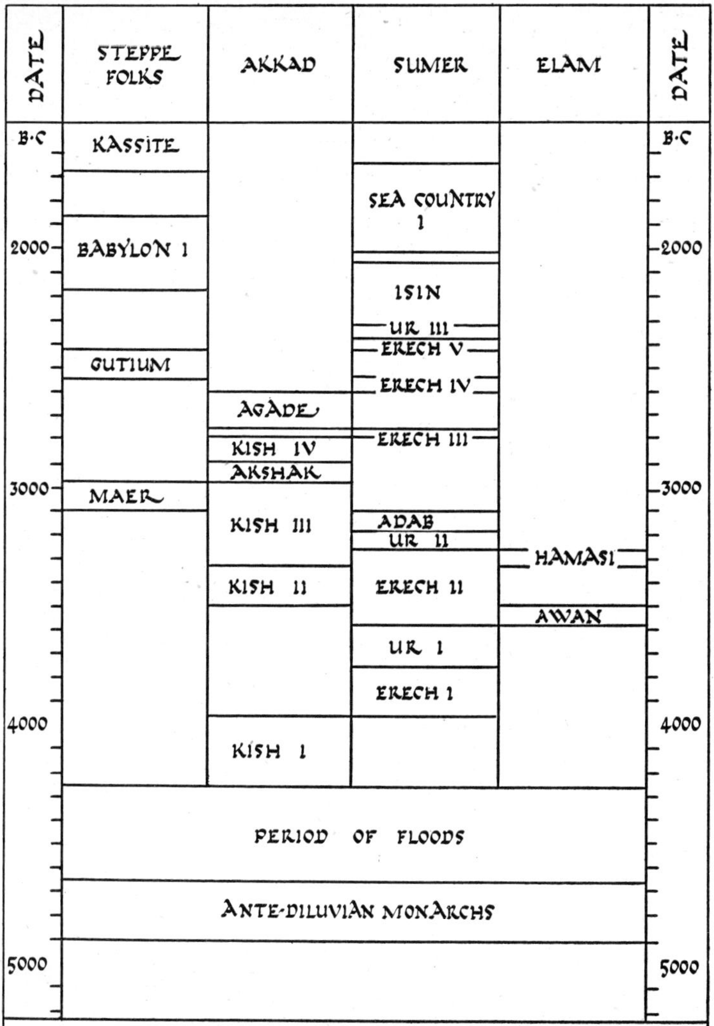

DATE B.C	STEPPE FOLKS	AKKAD	SUMER	ELAM	DATE B.C
	KASSITE				
			SEA COUNTRY 1		
2000	BABYLON 1				2000
			ISIN		
			UR III		
			ERECH V		
	GUTIUM		ERECH IV		
		AGADE			
		KISH IV	ERECH III		
		AKSHAK			
3000	MAER	KISH III	ADAB		3000
			UR II	HAMASI	
		KISH II	ERECH II	AWAN	
			UR I		
			ERECH I		
4000		KISH I			4000
	PERIOD OF FLOODS				
	ANTE-DILUVIAN MONARCHS				
5000					5000

Fig. 8. Chronological Chart of Mesopotamian dynasties.

Note. The chart reads, in order of time, from the bottom upwards.

Unlike the dwellers in Babylonia the Egyptians were not much interested in astronomy, and took little note even of eclipses of the sun. They were, however, accomplished growers of grain, and their fields were very dependent on the rich material brought down to them by the Nile floods. As this is an annual event of much regularity a calendar was all-important to them, and we shall see that at a very early date they had fixed a solar year with very fair accuracy. Yet it was not quite accurate, and it is this small lack of accuracy that has enabled us to obtain the astronomical evidence that we require.

The Egyptian year seems at first to have consisted of twelve months of thirty days each, but at an early date, which we believe we can fix with precision, they added five extra days, thus making their year consist of 365 days. But the solar year is nearly 365¼ days, and we provide for that quarter by adding one day to the month of February every fourth year or, as we call it, leap year. If we did not do this, Midsummer Day, which now always falls on 24 June, would every four years move on one day and would pass round the calendar, till after a period of 365¼ × 4 or 1,461 years it would return to its old place.

This is what happened in Egypt, and it was only later in the history of that land that this fact was fully understood and that it was realized that their calendar formed a cycle of 1,461 years, which they called a Sothic cycle. Sothis was the Egyptian name for the star Sirius, and at an early date they had been able to fix the longest day by observing the latest visible rising of Sirius or Sothis before the sunrise. This, known as the heliacal rising of Sirius, occurred on the first day of the month Thoth when the calendar was first adopted. Censorinus, writing in the third century of our era, says that the heliacal rising of Sirius coincided with the first day of Thoth in the year

Fig. 9. The Nile in flood.

A.D. 139. From this we conclude that a fresh Sothic cycle began that year and that the previous cycle began 1,461 years earlier, that is to say in 1321 B.C. Inscriptions tell us that in a certain year in the reign of Thothmes III the New Year festival fell on the twenty-eighth day of the eleventh month, from which it is possible to calculate that the year in question lay between 1474 and 1470. Again, in the ninth year of Amenhotep I the feast fell on the ninth day of the same month, so that the ninth year of that king fell between 1550 and 1546. Lastly, it has been possible to identify two New Moon festivals in the twenty-third and twenty-fourth years of Thothmes III. Calculating back from these dates it has been found that the accession of the eighteenth dynasty can be placed with fair precision in 1580 B.C. The previous cycles must have begun in 2781 and 4241 B.C.

In a papyrus found at Kahun it is stated that the heliacal rising of Sothis occurred on the first day of the month Pharmouthi in the seventh year of Senusret III, the fifth king of the twelfth dynasty, and reckoning back from this we find that this dynasty must have begun in 2000 B.C. This date has, however, presented difficulties to some Egyptologists, for if it be accepted the end of the thirteenth dynasty would have occurred in 1788 B.C., leaving only 208 years for the fourteenth to the seventeenth dynasties. Two solutions of the difficulty have been attempted.

Sir Flinders Petrie has taken the bold step of interpreting the Kahun papyrus as referring to a cycle earlier than that accepted by other Egyptologists, and so has added 1,461 years to their dates ; this leaves the interval between the thirteenth and the eighteenth dynasties at 1,669 years. Against this it has been argued that the number of dynasties and kings recorded does not warrant so long an interval. Hall has also pointed out, with much force, the near relationship of the art of the early

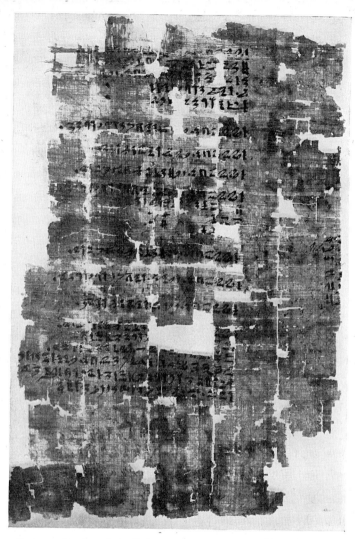

Fig. 10. Portion of the Kahun papyrus describing the heliacal rising of Sothis. Reproduced by the courtesy of Das Staatliche Museum, Berlin.

part of the eighteenth dynasty to that of the closing phase of the twelfth. An even more convincing argument comes from another source. As we shall see towards the close of this chapter Sir Arthur Evans has divided the culture which he has found at Knossos in Crete into nine periods, starting with the first evidence of metal ; the three middle periods he has termed respectively Middle Minoan I, II, and III, and the last of these is followed by the Late Minoan I period. He has shown that the objects found in the Second Middle Minoan deposits are contemporary with those of the twelfth dynasty in Egypt and to some extent with those of the early part of the thirteenth dynasty. On the other hand, the deposits of the First Late Minoan period are of the same date as the beginning of the eighteenth dynasty. It is Evans's considered opinion that the remains from the Third Middle Minoan period are so few in number and present so little change in style that it seems unreasonable to extend the period over more than four or five generations. This would lead us to believe that 208 years was an ample interval to allow between the thirteenth and eighteenth dynasties.

But Hall himself is not satisfied with the interval. He considers it too short to allow for all the kings whose reigns are known to us ; and so he wishes to lengthen the period by 200 years. This suggestion was first made in 1913 and was repeated ten years later in the *Cambridge Ancient History*. His arguments had such an effect upon his colleagues that the chronology adopted in that volume was based upon his views. We feel, however, that there are serious objections to this addition. The arguments that he himself has used against Petrie, and still more those of Evans, seem fatal to his proposed extension. In a time of admitted turmoil, with rival dynasties in the field, many monarchs may have ruled, or claimed to have ruled, in

Fig. 11. The Palermo Stele.

a very short space of time. Our chief objection, however, to Hall's amendment is that it entirely disregards the astronomical evidence of the Kahun papyrus on which he himself has set such store. We prefer, therefore, with Meyer, Breasted, Evans, and a host of others, to accept the year 2000 B.C. as being, with a possible error of a few years, the date of the accession of the twelfth dynasty.

For the period prior to the twelfth dynasty we have to depend on dead reckoning, now helped for part of the time by the Palermo Stele, and on estimating for the first intermediate period which falls between the sixth and eleventh dynasties.

Petrie estimates the time between the accession of Menes and the foundation of the twelfth dynasty at 2,100 years, Hall at 1,288, Breasted at 1,400, and Meyer at 1,315. Thus the date of Menes, according to these authorities, was Petrie 5500, Hall 3500, Breasted 3400, Meyer 3315, and Borchardt has added a fresh date, 4186 B.C., and Meyer a revised date 3197–8 B.C.

In Germany Borchardt's date was at first adopted by some of his colleagues, but it has now been abandoned by them. The *Cambridge Ancient History* has adopted Hall's, while Evans has utilized Meyer's. We feel that there is not much to choose between Meyer's last date and Breasted's, as they are separated by only two centuries. There are, however, so many small uncertainties in the estimates that have been made for the time preceding the twelfth dynasty, that we think it wiser for the present to adopt a round figure rather than one which claims a great precision. For this reason we are in this work adopting Breasted's date of 3400 B.C. as that of the accession of Menes, the founder of the first dynasty. In agreement with both Hall and Breasted we accept for the first adoption of the calendar the date 4241 B.C., believing with them that this is the earliest precise date that we have.

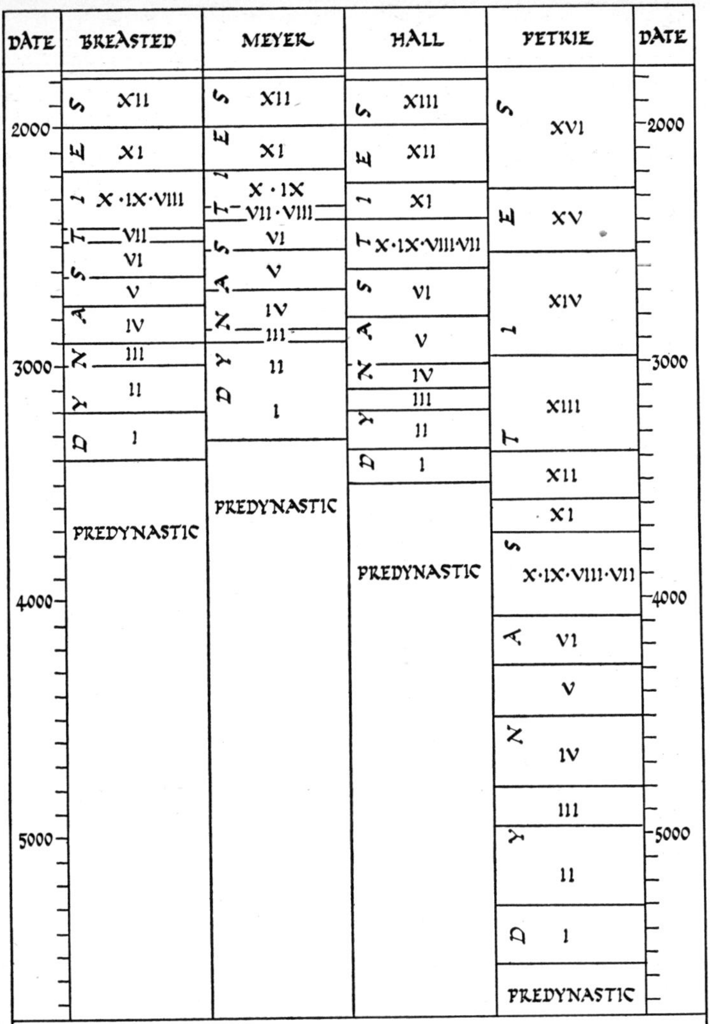

DATE	BREASTED	MEYER	HALL	PETRIE	DATE
2000	XII	XII	XIII	XVI	2000
	XI	XI	XII		
	X·IX·VIII	X·IX·VII·VIII	XI	XV	
	VII	VI	X·IX·VIII·VII		
	VI	V	VI	XIV	
	V	IV	V		
	IV	III	IV	XIII	
3000	III	II	III		3000
	II	I	II	XII	
	I		I	XI	
	PREDYNASTIC	PREDYNASTIC		X·IX·VIII·VII	
			PREDYNASTIC	VI	
4000				V	4000
				IV	
				III	
5000				II	5000
				I	
				PREDYNASTIC	

(DYNASTIES labelled vertically in each of the Breasted, Meyer, Hall, and Petrie columns)

Fig. 12. Chart of the early dynasties of Egypt

Note. The chart reads, in order of time, from the bottom upwards.

We must now turn our attention to Crete, where a wonderful civilization has been revealed to us by the spade of Sir Arthur Evans and many other explorers who have followed in his footsteps. From the time when metal first appears among the remains discovered until the destruction of the civilization by invaders armed with weapons of iron many successive stages have been found of this civilization, which Evans has appropriately termed Minoan, after Minos the legendary king of Crete. Evans at an early stage recognized three main phases, which he termed Early, Middle, and Late Minoan, and he found each of these capable of subdivision into three minor periods, which he has called I, II, and III. Still later some of these lesser periods have been further subdivided into *a* and *b*. Few inscriptions have been found and these only in the later phases; since these still remain undecipherable and seem, for the most part, to consist of lists of stores, we cannot use them as a basis for chronology.

On the other hand, the relations between Crete and Egypt were intimate throughout the Minoan epoch, and it is not uncommon to find objects of Egyptian workmanship in the stratified deposits of Crete, while occasional Minoan objects have been discovered in Egypt. It has thus not been difficult to find several definite synchronisms. Stone bowls, dating from the early dynasties, are not uncommon among the deposits of Early Minoan I, though some of these, Evans thinks, may be late predynastic. Objects more typical of the Old Kingdom, the fourth to the sixth dynasties, occur in Early Minoan II. Early objects of the twelfth dynasty make their appearance before the close of Middle Minoan I and appear more frequently, sometimes with articles dating from the thirteenth dynasty, in Middle Minoan II. Connexions between Late Minoan I and the eighteenth dynasty are frequent. On this basis Evans has drawn up a chart which we give below.

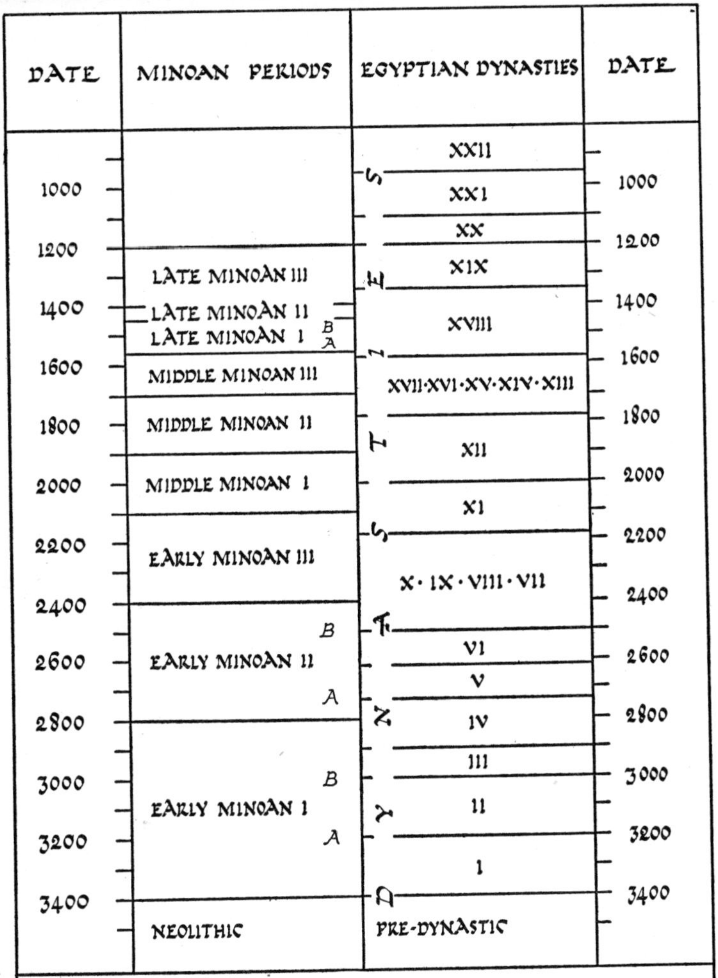

DATE	MINOAN PERIODS	EGYPTIAN DYNASTIES	DATE
		XXII	
1000		XXI	1000
1200		XX	1200
1400	LATE MINOAN III	XIX	1400
	LATE MINOAN II	XVIII	
	LATE MINOAN I B A		
1600	MIDDLE MINOAN III	XVII·XVI·XV·XIV·XIII	1600
1800	MIDDLE MINOAN II	XII	1800
2000	MIDDLE MINOAN I		2000
		XI	
2200	EARLY MINOAN III		2200
2400		X·IX·VIII·VII	2400
2600	EARLY MINOAN II B	VI	2600
	A	V	
2800		IV	2800
3000		III	3000
	EARLY MINOAN I B	II	
3200	A		3200
		I	
3400			3400
	NEOLITHIC	PRE-DYNASTIC	

Fig. 13. Chart of Minoan Periods.

Note. The chart reads, in order of time, from the bottom upwards.

Lastly, it has been possible to bring the successive cultures in the Aegean islands and on the mainland of Greece into line with those of Crete and to use a parallel terminology, with the terms Cycladic and Helladic in the place of Minoan. Thus Early Cycladic I denotes the culture in the Cyclades and other Aegean islands contemporary with Early Minoan I in Crete, while Middle Helladic II represents the civilization on the mainland of Greece while Middle Minoan II flourished at Knossos. Elsewhere in Asia Minor and Europe the chronology used is arrived at by synchronisms with those already mentioned, and attempts will be made to explain and to justify the dates used in this work as occasion offers.

BOOKS

BREASTED, J. H.   *A History of Egypt* (New York, 1912), Ch. II.
Cambridge Ancient History, vol. i (London, 1923), Ch. IV, iii.
EVANS, A. J.   *The Palace of Minos at Knossos, Crete* (London, 1922).
HALL, H. R.   *The Ancient History of the Near East* (London, 1913), Ch. I.

3

Sumer and Akkad

WE have seen in the last part that the lower lands of Mesopotamia were settled at an early date, and we have traced the fortunes of their inhabitants until the fall of the first dynasty of Ur about 3575 B.C. We know of many cities in the plain at this time : Susa at the foot of the Zagros range, Awan and Hamasi, sometimes spelt Khamazi, at unidentified sites at no great distance from it. Ur and Eridu were then on the Persian Gulf near one of the mouths of the Euphrates, while Lagash, sometimes called Shirpurla, and Umma lay on either side of another mouth ; Erech and Larsa lay a few miles up the river.

The site of Maer has not been identified, but it is known that it lay on the Euphrates, near its junction with the Khabur, about 200 miles above Bagdad. Akshak, the Opis of later days, was on the Tigris, about fifty miles above Bagdad, while

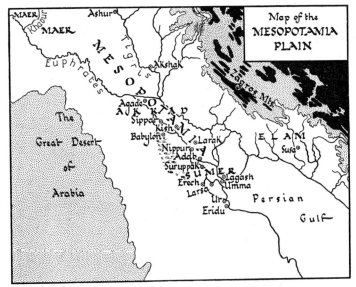

FIG. 14.

Sippar was on the Euphrates, almost opposite that city, with Agade, which was founded later, a few miles to the south. Farther down, near the site of Babylon, was Kish, while farther still were Nippur, to the east of which lay Larak, Adab, and Šuruppak. The site of Badtibira, the seat of one of the ante-diluvian monarchies, has not yet been identified, but the word *tibira* is thought to mean ' metal-workers '. It is also worth noting that the whole of the area described, from Maer to Susa, is about the size of Great Britain.

The first dynasty of Ur seems to have fallen before an invasion from the east of the Tigris by a people whom we conjecture to have been Elamites; these ruled the land from Awan until about 3500 B.C., when they were driven back by the men of Kish who established the second dynasty of that city. We know nothing of this dynasty but the names of seven of its eight kings. They seem to have kept the Elamites at bay about 3320 B.C. Hadanis, king of Hamasi or Khamazi, suc-

FIG. 15.   Mace-head of Mesilim.

ceeded in establishing himself as ruler over the southern territories, though, if we are right in our conjectures, he failed to conquer the states near the mouths of the Euphrates, over which Enugduanna or Ensag-kus-anna, king of Erech, established his sway. Kish seems to have remained independent for a time, until Enbi-Ashtar its king was conquered by Ensag-kus-anna. At the death of Hadanis, about 3295 B.C., the rule of Hamasi came to an end, and Erech became the leading city. It seems probable that Ensag-kus-anna died about the same time and that his successor transferred the seat of government to Ur, thus founding the second dynasty of that city. This ruled until 3187 B.C., and it is to the closing years of its rule that we are inclined to refer two kings of Kish, who are not mentioned in the royal lists.

Mesilim, the first of these, seems for a time to have resumed his suzerainty over the eastern section of the valley, for we

Fig. 16.   Pottery from Cemetery A at Kish.

find that he set up a stele to fix the boundary between the lands of Lagash and Umma.   He continued to interest himself in the affairs of Lagash and built a temple for Ningirsu, the god of that city.   On that occasion he dedicated to the god a fine lime-stone mace-head, eight inches high and five and a half in diameter, on which is an inscription mentioning Lugal-shagengur, the patesi or priestly magistrate of Lagash.   Another king of Kish, Urzaged, who dedicated a stone vase to the god Enlil and his consort Ninlil in Nippur, was probably his immediate successor.

It is to about this date, or perhaps to the next century, that we must relegate the cemetery, known as Cemetery A, which has lately been uncovered at Kish by the joint expedition from Oxford and Chicago. A very full account of this cemetery and of the contents of its graves has been compiled by its excavator, Ernest Mackay, and issued by the Field Museum of Chicago.

Here were found thirty-eight graves containing skeletons in a slightly contracted position with a great wealth of grave goods. These included jugs with faces on the handles, pedestalled bowls, vases and pots of many different forms. Besides these there were a great variety of copper implements and tools, necklaces of beads, amulets and *Cardium* shells containing white, light-green, blue, red, and black pigments. The bones were not in a good condition, but five skulls were sufficiently preserved to enable them to be measured. These show both long and short heads or intermediate forms, so that the population of the city was clearly of mixed origin.

On the fall of the second dynasty of Ur, about 3187 B.C., the primacy passed to the city of Adab. The royal list gives only one king, Lugal-mundu, who is said to have ruled for ninety years, but we may conjecture that several successors shared this period with him. On the site of the city of Adab has been found an archaic statuette, which represents Lugal-dalu, king of Adab. Another king, Mebasi, is known from an inscription on a vase. The dynasty of Adab came to an end about 3097 B.C., owing to an invasion from without.

For the period up to this time we may recognize three groups of people. East of the lower Tigris and on the foot-hills of the

Zagros were the peoples of Susa, Awan, and Hamasi. These were the people responsible for the second civilization of Susa, and, apparently, only distantly connected with those of Susa I; they seem to have been the people known later as Elamites. Between the Tigris and the Euphrates, and especially around

FIG. 17. Pottery from Susa II.

the mouths of the latter river, were the Sumerian city states, while to the north, at Kish and perhaps Akshak and Sippar, lived a mixed population. The names of some of their kings seem to indicate that there was a considerable Sumerian element, while other names have a decidedly Semitic appearance. We have suggested in an earlier part that the Southern

Steppe-folk were originally the speakers of the Semitic languages, but we have also put forward the idea that in North Syria these steppe-folk had mingled with the hill-folk to their north. It is quite possible, therefore, that the Semitic-speaking population of these more northern towns contained these steppe- and hill-folk as well as Sumerian elements.

Each Sumerian city, and probably those farther north also, had its presiding deity with his consort, temple, and priests. One of these priests was known as a *Patesi*, and later by the Semitic invaders as an *Ishakku*. He appears to have been a priestly magistrate or judge, and he governed the city and its lands as vice-regent of the deity. Only when he had extended his rule to include neighbouring cities did the patesi adopt the title of *Lugal* or king.

Away to the north-west, on the desert and its margin, dwelt a number of Southern Steppe-folk, in some places mixed with hillmen from the north. Of these, we believe, were composed the inhabitants of the city or territory of Maer, which lay somewhere near the confluence of the Khabur and the Euphrates. The first king that we know of, who seems to have reigned during the closing years of the dynasty of Adab, bore the name Ila-Shamash, ' Shamash is my god '. This is Semitic. He or his immediate successor seems to have made a great raid southwards and brought the whole of the valley under his rule about 3097 B.C. It is curious, however, that of the six kings in the royal list four certainly, and perhaps the other two whose names are imperfectly known, bore Sumerian names. It has been thought that, perhaps, the people of Maer were backward in civilization and illiterate, and that they employed Sumerians as scribes and minor officials. These scribes would, very likely, give Sumerian names to the Semitic kings when writing them on clay tablets. Little is known of the doings of the kings of

Maer ; a decapitated limestone figure of one of them is in the British Museum. The rule of the later kings was weak, at any rate in the south, and there are signs that their times were troublous.

Fig. 18.   Limestone figure of a king of Maer.

We have more than once mentioned Lagash, hitherto governed by patesis. Shortly before the year 3000 B.C. there arose a citizen who claimed the title of king, from which we may gather that he had enabled his city to throw off the suzerainty of Maer. This was Ur-Nina, the son of Gunidu and grandson of Guroar. Neither of the last named seems to have held any official appointment, so we must assume that Ur-Nina was a private citizen who came to the rescue of his state and freed it from foreign domination. He seems to have been content with this, for the numerous records that he has left make no mention of wars of conquest, while his relations with the neighbouring Sumerian states seem to have been uniformly friendly. He spent most of his time restoring old temples and building new ones in honour of the numerous deities worshipped in Lagash, and in making friendly pilgrimages to the shrines of the patron deities of other Sumerian cities. He also cut many canals, presumably for irrigation, and built many granaries, usually within temple precincts.

Ur-Nina had a daughter, Lidda, and at least four sons, Akurgal, Lugal-ezen, Anikurra, and Muninnikurta. Akurgal seems to have been associated with his father during the final years of the latter's reign, and in due course succeeded to the sole rule of the city. His reign was short and uneventful, and the peace that had distinguished his father's time was broken only once by a brief quarrel with the neighbouring city of Umma across the river.

Akurgal left two sons, Eannatum and Enannatum I; the former succeeded his father as patesi or king of Lagash. Like his grandfather he spent much of the early part of his reign in building temples and adding to their lands. It would seem that about this time the power of the kings of Maer still further diminished, and rival dynasties, anxious for their independence, were arising in Kish and Akshak as well as Lagash. The latter under Eannatum enlarged the bounds of its territories by the annexation of Ur, Erech, Larsa, and a number of minor states. Then in his piety Eannatum bestowed upon the god Ningirsu a tract of alluvial land known as Gu-edin. This act was resented by Ush, patesi of Umma, who claimed that the land in question lay within the bounds formerly laid down by Mesilim and determined by the stele that he had set up. So one day, assisted it would seem by the king of Kish, Ush removed the stele of Mesilim and led out the men of Umma into Gu-edin, where they cut the crops and returned to their city with much booty.

FIG. 19. Plaque representing Ur-Nina, king of Lagash, and his family.

Eannatum paused for a time before undertaking reprisals, then fell upon the men of Umma, slew large numbers of them, deposed Ush, and eventually concluded a treaty of peace with Enakalli, whom he had appointed patesi in his place.

The defeat of Umma was resented by the king of Kish, and he sought help from Zuzu, king of Akshak, and their suzerain the king of Maer. The three armies laid siege to

Lagash, but were quickly defeated by Eannatum, who slew the king of Kish, chased Zuzu all the way back to Akshak, and finally defeated the king of Maer. While this expedition was

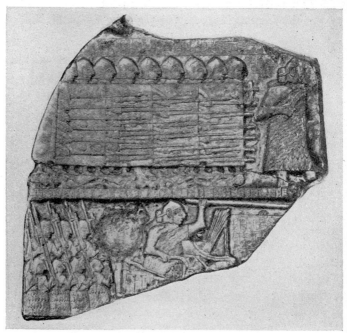

Fig. 20.   Portion of the stele of the vultures.

going on and Eannatum with his army was absent in the north, the Elamites crossed the river and attacked Lagash. Eannatum, however, returned in time to drive the invaders back across the Tigris to their own territory. It would seem that the defeat of the king of Maer brought the over-lordship of that dynasty to an end, and, if that was so, we may consider these wars of Eannatum as having taken place about 2961 B.C.

The account of these campaigns has been pieced together mainly from inscriptions on the famous ' Stele of the Vultures ', fragments of which are at the Louvre and the British Museum. The various statements are scattered, but have been well summarized by Mr. L. W. King, and the above seems to be the only intelligible interpretation of them. After this Eannatum seems to have led as peaceful a life as his predecessors, and to have occupied himself in cutting fresh irrigation canals and building a large reservoir. He died childless, and was succeeded by his brother Enannatum I.

The expedition of Eannatum was, as we have seen, fatal to the overlordship of the kings of Maer, and for a time the land was shared among several separate states. Elam still held most of the land to the east of the Tigris, Lagash ruled the Sumerian cities of the south, Kish may still have had some predominance among its neighbours; but the chief power in the north now fell to Akshak, whose king Unzi, successor apparently to Zuzu, claimed the overlordship. Judging by the names of the three first kings of this dynasty, the royal house was Sumerian, but we know nothing of their doings. The reign of Enannatum I was short and on the whole uneventful, and he continued, like his predecessors, to embellish the temples of the gods. Only once was the peace of Lagash disturbed. Enakalli, whom Eannatum had made patesi of Umma, died and was succeeded by his son Urlumma, who was not of an equally friendly disposition. One day with the men of Umma he overthrew the stele of Mesilim, broke it in pieces and cast it on a fire, and did the same with the stele which Eannatum had set up. Then they ravaged the fields of Lagash and attacked the city. Enannatum I fought them outside the walls and was only partly successful in defeating them. The opposing forces, however, came eventually to a truce, and the peace was not further disturbed during this reign. Enannatum I had two sons, Entemena and Lummurdur, and he was succeeded by the former.

Scarcely had Entemena ascended the throne when Urlumma attacked again. This time the king of Lagash met the forces of Umma outside the city in the fields of Gu-edin, defeated them, ravaged their city, slew Urlumma, and brought Umma finally under the sway of Lagash. He then appointed Ili, priest of a neighbouring town, to act as patesi. After that he proceeded to consolidate his dominions which now included all the Sumerian city-states by the mouths of the Euphrates. He cleaned out the ditches and brought back under cultivation the land ravaged by the men of Umma ; he also annexed some of the territory of Karker, a neighbouring village. Like his predecessor he was mainly engaged in improving the irrigation ditches and in making an additional reservoir.

He was succeeded on the throne by his son Enannatum II, of whom very little is known and with whom the dynasty of Ur-Nina came to an end. For some years the city was ruled by patesis, of whom the names of three are known to us. The first of these was Enetarzi, chief priest of Ningirsu, who governed the city for about four years. He was followed by Enlitarzi, another chief priest of Ningirsu, who ruled for about five years, when he gave up his post to his son Lugal-anda, who held it for at least seven years.

We have seen that a series of kings of Akshak, some bearing Sumerian names, had been claiming the overlordship since about 2961 B.C. The fourth and fifth of these, curiously enough, had Semitic names, which suggests that a fresh family had come into power about 2919 B.C. These fresh monarchs, perhaps, succeeded in making their rule felt in Lagash after the death of Enannatum II, thus reducing its rulers to the rank of

FIG. 21.   Silver vase dedicated to Ningirsu by Entemena.

patesi. About 2875 B.C., however, Akshak came under the rule of Gimil-Sin, in whom we may recognize the first king of the fourth dynasty of Kish.

It appears that some years earlier Kish had revolted from the rule of Akshak, and a female wine-seller named Azag-Bau, who appears on the Weld-Blundell prism as Kug-Bau, made herself queen and reigned in Kish for a very long time ; several of the lists credit her with a reign of 100 years and describe this

FIG. 22.   Impression of a seal of Lugal-anda.

time as the third dynasty of Kish.   That she was a person of outstanding character is clear from allusions to her in much later documents.   Though we cannot accept the great length of her reign, she was undoubtedly the mother of Gimil-Sin, the first king of the fourth dynasty of Kish.   Azag-Bau is said to have acted as queen-regent during the twenty-five years that Gimil-Sin ruled in Kish, and during part, at least, of the short reign of her grandson Ur-Ilbaba.   The fourth dynasty of Kish ruled until 2777 B.C., when it gave way to the third dynasty of Erech.

During the latter part of the overlordship of the fourth

dynasty of Kish, Lagash again rebelled and established its independence. Urukagina became patesi and, after a year, called himself king, which was equivalent to denying the overlordship of Kish. He found affairs at Lagash in a very bad condition, the people over-taxed, and both priests and officials corrupt. Immediately he instituted reforms. He cut down the

FIG. 23. Tombs at Lagash.

civil service and reduced the emoluments of the priesthood, especially the fees for burial. He promulgated a number of laws for the benefit of his people, cleaned out the irrigation ditches, and constructed another large reservoir. Under his rule Lagash began to prosper, but, as usual in such circumstances, aroused the antagonism of the neighbouring city of Umma.

Here Ukush the patesi had lately died, and his son Lugal-zaggisi wished to improve the fortunes of his city. He attacked Lagash, defeated Urukagina, and annexed the city. Soon afterwards he conquered Erech, which he made the seat of his government, and started off to reduce the whole of Mesopotamia. About 2777 B.C. he conquered Kish, bringing the fourth dynasty to an end, and for twenty-five years he ruled the land as sole monarch of the third dynasty of Erech.

Thus constant wars were waged for the supremacy of the land between the rivers, and one city after another held the overlordship. Yet all through we may notice three great elements at work. Near the Persian Gulf were the Sumerian cities—the richest and most civilized of all. Northward from Babylon lay the region of Akkad, the cities of which contained a Sumerian element, enjoyed Sumerian laws and civilization, and were sometimes ruled by Sumerian monarchs. In this area, in which Kish was the most prominent city, the population was mixed. We have already seen reason for believing that some of its inhabitants were hillmen from the Anatolian highlands, but as time went on there seems to have been an ever-increasing infiltration of Southern Steppe-folk from the desert. This was particularly marked during the dominance of the dynasty of Maer. Meanwhile, across the Tigris the third element, the Elamites, were ever on the watch to raid the rich cities and their lands when any of them showed signs of weakness.

Lugal-zaggisi had ruled the land for twenty-five years, when there arose at Kish an adventurer, whose exploits were long remembered in the land between the rivers. This was Sharru-kin-ilubani, ' a legitimate king is verily created ', popularly known as Sargon of Agade.

The early history of Sargon is wrapped in mystery, though legend has been busy creating for him an interesting origin. One of the royal lists says, ' At Agade Sharru-kin-ilubani, a gardener and cup-bearer of Ur-Ilbaba, having been made king, ruled for fifty-five years '. Ur-Ilbaba was a king of Kish who had died more than eighty years before the accession of Sargon, but it has been thought that the latter was an official in a temple erected to Ur-Ilbaba's memory. One tradition says that his father's name was Laipum and that he was brought up among cattle, which suggests that his origin was rather on the steppes than in the city. Another story relates that his mother was

Fig. 24. Cylinder said to be of Sargon of Agade.

of humble origin and his father unknown, and that he was born in concealment at Azupirani on the Euphrates. His mother cast him adrift on the river in a reed basket, where he was found and reared by Akki, an irrigator, who brought him up as a gardener. In this legend we recognize the story told of many deliverers and founders of empires, such as Cyrus, Moses, Perseus, Cypselus, and Romulus.

No sooner had he raised a rebellion, and in 2752 B.C. assumed the power at Kish, than he attacked Lugal-zaggisi, who summoned to his aid the governors of fifty cities. He defeated the coalition and carried Lugal-zaggisi in fetters to Nippur. Later he attacked Ur and destroyed its walls, and the following year reduced to subjection Lagash and its neighbours, though Umma was the last to capitulate. Then he attacked Susa, overran the cities of Elam, and incorporated the whole of that region in his kingdom, which now included the whole of the shore at the head of the Persian Gulf.

In his third year Sargon led his armies up the Euphrates, conquered the whole of North Syria, and reached the shores of the Mediterranean. He is said to have crossed that sea, but whether to Cyprus or to the shores of Cilicia is uncertain. On his return he founded the city of Agade, which from now on gave its name to Upper Mesopotamia, which was called Akkad. He built it on the model of Babylon, which seems to have been a city of special sanctity, though this is the earliest occasion on which mention of it has been found. An inscription on one of his statues at Nippur states that his kingdom included the cedar forests, presumably of Lebanon, and the silver mines, which have been identified with those in the Taurus near the Cilician gates.

After this for a time he had peace, and set to work to organize his great possessions. It was during this time that there was composed an official survey of his dominions, a late copy of which, made by an Assyrian scribe, was recently found at Assur. In this document we find another allusion to the Cedar-land and this passage which has been much quoted : ' To KUGA-KI (or KU-KI) and KAPTARA, countries beyond the Upper Sea, DILMUN and MAGANNA, countries beyond the Lower Sea, and the countries from the rising to the setting of the sun, which Sargon the king conquered with his hand.'

The Lower Sea is clearly the Persian Gulf, and we have already seen that Dilmun was somewhere beside it. The Upper Sea is no less unmistakably the Mediterranean ; Kaptara, the Caphtor of the Bible, without doubt is Crete ; but the identification of Kuga-ki or Ku-ki is a matter of dispute. Sayce, following several Continental authorities, considers that Ku means tin, and so Ku-ki means the Tin-land ; from this he argues that Spain is indicated. Langdon translates Ku as copper and identifies Ku-ki with Cyprus, the κύπρος of the Greeks, though, as we have seen, this interpretation raises difficulties.

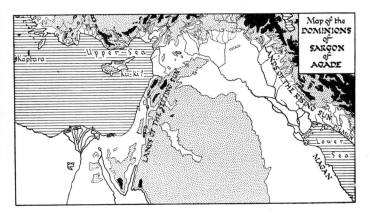

FIG. 25.

Once the peace of the kingdom was disturbed by an Elamite revolt, which was easily quelled, but as the king grew old his subjects became dissatisfied with his rule. On one occasion all the cities revolted and attacked Agade, but the old king led out his army and defeated them. He also undertook an expedition to the north against new tribes which had approached his frontiers. At length in 2697 B.C. he died, leaving several sons, Rimush or Urumush, who succeeded him, Ibarim and Amal-Ishdagal and, it is thought, several others.

No sooner was the old king dead than the cities revolted

again, and during the early years of his reign Rimush had to reduce to subjection the Sumerian cities and the land of Elam. After a reign of nine years he died and was succeeded by Manishtissu, who is believed to have been his brother. His experience was the same, but he soon put down all rebellions

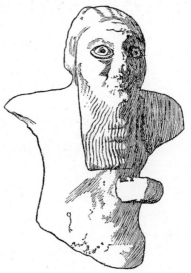

FIG. 26.   Alabaster statue of Manishtissu, dedicated by a high official to the god Naruti.

and reigned, apparently in peace, for fifteen years. During his time Engilsa was patesi of Lagash and Kurshesh of Umma.

On his death he was succeeded by another brother, Naram-Sin, whose reputation was nearly as great as that of his father Sargon. He experienced the usual revolt of the Sumerian cities and that of those of Akkad as well, while the Elamites again gave trouble. All were, however, successfully subdued, and Naram-Sin spent much of his time in peaceful administra-

FIG. 27.   Stele of Naram-Sin, king of Agade, representing the king and
his allies in triumph over their enemies.

tion and building temples. He seems to have received divine honours during his lifetime, a custom that soon grew more common. He appointed Sumerian patesis in the Sumerian cities, but in Elam the cities were put under magistrates with Semitic names. He had several sons who governed parts of his kingdom, but all of these seem to have died before the close of his reign, which lasted for thirty-eight years.

He was succeeded by Shargalishari, the son of Dati-Enlil, and apparently grandson of his predecessor. He had the same trouble with his subjects on his accession, but established his power successfully. Towards the close of his reign he had trouble, too, with the new-comers on his northern border, in the district of Gutium, though he succeeded in keeping them at bay. After a reign of twenty-four years he died, the last scion of the house of Sargon, and there followed a period of anarchy. Four kings ruled successively in three years, then the throne passed to Dudu, who held it for twenty-one, and then to Gimil-durul, who reigned for fifteen more. Nothing is known about these two last monarchs of the dynasty of Agade, and after the death of the last in 2571 B.C. the power passed again to the Sumerian city of Erech.

BOOKS

DELAPORTE, L. *Mesopotamia* (London, 1925).
HALL, H. R. *The Ancient History of the Near East* (London, 1912).
KING, L. W. *A History of Sumer and Akkad* (London, 1910).
LANGDON, S. *Oxford Editions of Cuneiform Texts*, vol. ii (Oxford, 1923).
The Cambridge Ancient History, vol. i (Cambridge, 1923).

4

The Old Kingdom of Egypt

In the last part we dealt with the civilization that developed in the Nile valley in what are known as predynastic times. Our evidence was archaeological, and we built up the story from the evidence supplied by pots, flint knives, and copper pins. Even in the earliest phases of the dynastic period we have passed from the prehistoric to the historic, for writing was known and we have a few inscriptions. We have also lists of kings, some of them compiled before the Old Kingdom came to an end, and these give the names of the rulers back to the beginning of the dynastic period. We have reason, too, for believing that had one of these lists come down to us whole we should have found in it the names of a number of pre-dynastic monarchs.

The lists of kings vary in date and in value. That compiled by Manetho about 300 B.C. was evidently based on earlier information, but we are dependent on extracts made from it by later Greek writers, who have miscopied the names until many of them are unrecognizable. Manetho's lists were pro-bably copied from two lists composed early in the nineteenth dynasty, between 1350 and 1250 B.C. These are the royal lists of Abydos and Sakkara ; both are accurate as far back as the fourth dynasty, but the names of the earlier kings have been inaccurately copied. More valuable than these is the Turin papyrus, compiled about the same time ; unfortunately this is in fragments, otherwise many of our difficulties would be solved. For the early dynasties reliable information can be obtained only from contemporary documents, which are few in number, and from the Palermo stone. This was one of a number of monumental stelae set up during the fifth dynasty, between 2750 and 2625 B.C. These contained records of every regnal year from the beginning of the first dynasty and included the names of many of the predynastic kings.

We have seen reason for thinking that the art of picture-writing arose in the Delta early in predynastic times, but, since

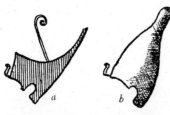

in that region deep digging has been impossible so far owing to the waterlogged state of the soil, no actual evidence of this has been discovered. We have, however, a few short inscriptions from Upper Egypt, which date from the closing phase of the predynastic period. The symbols at this time differed somewhat from those in use later, for the writing

FIG. 28. *a* The red crown of Lower Egypt, and *b* the white crown of Middle Egypt.

was still in a state of evolution. By the time of the fourth dynasty the system was fully developed, and from that time on varied little.

At the close of the predynastic period there were two distinct peoples occupying the Delta, as well as the aborigines whom they had conquered and perhaps absorbed. Those immigrants from Syria, and perhaps ultimately from the Anatolian highlands, who had introduced the cultivation of grain and worshipped Osiris, had occupied the centre, but had by this time been driven south of Cairo. Their former capital had been at Buto, south-east of Rosetta. To the east were the goatherds, the worshippers of Anzety. To the west were the Libyan tribe, the Tehenu, a group of Southern Steppe-folk who had long been settled on the western margin of the Delta, where they cultivated the olive. For some little time before the close of the predynastic period these people had occupied the western part of the Delta, and had established their capital at Sais, just south of Buto, driving the grain-growers southwards, and before the close of the period their rulers claimed to be kings of Lower Egypt, and had adopted as a crown a red cap, which had been an emblem of Neith, the goddess of Sais.

In Middle Egypt, between Cairo and Assiût, the grain-growers had established another kingdom, the capital of which seems to have been at Aphroditopolis, just south of Cairo. Here was the *Het-Insi*, the house of the *Insi*, as these kings were called. It seems that it was these monarchs, rather than the kings of Upper Egypt, who wore the white crown, which in later days was combined with the red crown to form the diadem of the Pharaohs. It is clear from certain signs on the Palermo stone that ten kings had ruled over Middle and Lower Egypt before the close of the predynastic period ; though their names are missing, ten signs of the double crown have been noted by Breasted on a fragment of the stone. We know, however, something of the last six kings of Lower Egypt, who may, perhaps, be the last six of the ten in question. The names of the first and last of these are undecipherable, but those of the remaining four are Tiu, Thesh, Hsekiu, and Uaznar. Between Assiût and Abydos the valley was occupied by another tribe, who were worshippers of the pig, known as Set ; the hippopotamus was also sacred among these people.

The southernmost part of Egypt, between Abydos and Assuan, had for long been dominated by the stone-bowl people who had perhaps come from the Arabian Desert, and it was, perhaps, a family of these who had established their rule on the upper reaches of the Nile below the first cataract. Some Egyptologists think that towards the close of the predynastic period a fresh wave of invaders came from the shores of the Red Sea, while Egyptian tradition brings the new-comers from Nubia. On the other hand, Newberry has given reasons for thinking that they had come up the river many centuries earlier from the western corner of the Delta.

Some have argued that these people, who founded the first dynasty and had a falcon for their emblem, had come from the Red Sea and ultimately from some place on the coast of Arabia or the Persian Gulf. They point out that during the closing phases of the Late Predynastic period some of the Egyptians used mace-heads and cylinder-seals almost exactly similar to those found somewhat later in Mesopotamia, though soon after the beginning of the first dynasty their use ceased. They note, too, that on the knife-handle from Gebel El Arak, described in the last part, the decorative motives are Sumerian rather than Egyptian in style, while there are representations of boats with tall prow and stern but quite unlike the river-boats of the Nile ; moreover, on several pots of this date appears the figure of a bird killing a fish or serpent. Frankfort has figured a vase found at Lagash, later in date, it is true, by more than a thousand years, on which appear this type of boat and the bird-with-fish symbol ; he has claimed that both these motives are Sumerian.

Crawford has argued recently from this and similar evidence that these dynastic Egyptians, and the Sumerians as well, came from Arabia. He cites a description recently given by Major Cheeseman of the Al Murra, a pagan tribe, who have only recently acquired the Arabic or indeed any Semitic speech, and whom he met with near Jabrin in Arabia. Major Cheeseman is quoted as having said, ' The Al Murra type of face reminds me of features to be seen on early Sumerian sculptures '.

If these arguments carry any weight it is more probable that

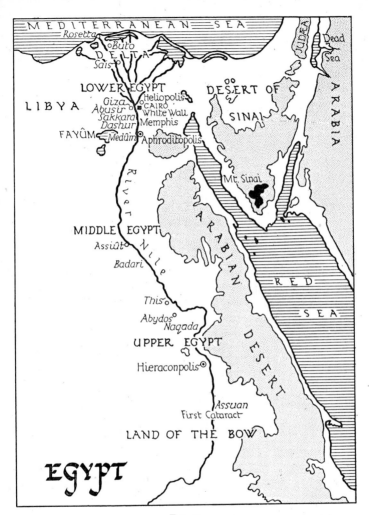

FIG. 29.

the common cradle of the dynastic Egyptians and of the Sumerians was somewhere on the Persian Gulf, where the latter placed Dilmun, their Paradise. In this connexion we may mention that evidence of an early culture, in which copper was known, has been reported recently from the Bahrein Islands in the Persian Gulf; this, however, turns out to be of much later date.

Petrie has suggested that these Falcon-folk came from the

FIG. 30.   Boat and bird with fish on an Egyptian vase.

first settlement at Susa, and Miss Murray has pointed out that certain human figures, represented on first dynasty objects, are shown with pigtails. Against this it may be argued that the first settlement at Susa came to an end nearly a thousand years before the foundation of the first dynasty, while Frankfort suggests that the pigtails noted by Miss Murray are unlike those of the early dwellers at Susa and more nearly resemble the sidelocks worn by certain Libyan tribes. On the other hand, a drawing of a presumed Sumerian, recently found by Professor Langdon in a very early layer at Kish, depicts him with a similar sidelock. If Miss Murray's contention is correct

FIG. 31.   Boat and bowl with fish on a vase from Lagash.

and these are true pigtails, there remains the possibility that the Falcon-folk came by sea from North Syria, and passed up the Nile as Newberry has suggested.

FIG. 32.   Mace-head of ' the Scorpion '.

Whatever be the true explanation, a line of kings ruled at Abydos or Naqada ; they were worshippers of the Falcon, which they called Horus, and this name was added to that of their kings. The names of only two of these kings can as yet be made out with certainty, one called Ro, who is thought to have been contemporary with Uaznar, and one who is called ' the

Scorpion '. The latter seems to have begun the series of conquests which ended in the unification of Egypt ; he certainly conquered the middle area, for he is called *Insi*, but he seems to have failed to subdue the Delta.

The Scorpion was succeeded by Narmer or Narmerza, who is usually identified with the traditional Menes. Some Egyptologists have suggested that the deeds attributed to Menes were performed not only by Narmer, but by the Scorpion his predecessor and by Aha Men his successor. Tradition asserts that he ruled at Thinis or This, which was close to Abydos. He succeeded to the kingdoms of Upper and Middle Egypt and wore the white crown of the latter. Then he attacked the Delta, defeated the Tehenu, captured Sais, and married the heiress of the defeated monarch. Thus Egypt became one kingdom. Aha, his successor, is found wearing the double crown, and is said to have extended the kingdom right up to the first cataract. Their successors had more than once to defend the southern frontier, known as ' the land of the bow ', but otherwise the remaining kings ruled in peace. Merpeba, the sixth king, fixed the seat of government at the city of the ' White Wall ', a few miles south of Cairo, and close to the later capital of Memphis, which arose in due course outside its walls.

The first dynasty gave way to the second about 3200 B.C. This dynasty is stated by tradition to have been Thinite like the first, but there are good reasons for thinking that its kings were northerners, and it has been suggested that the Horus name of the second king, Reneb Kakau, bears some resemblance to the type of name used at this time in Mesopotamia. This leads us to suspect that the grain-growers of the Middle Nile, of North Syrian origin, who had been conquered by the Scorpion, had now at length asserted their supremacy. Tradition relates that there were eight kings of this dynasty, but traces of the first six only have been found. Of these the second, Reneb, or Nebra, bears a name compounded of the name of the sun-god Re, which suggests that he had connexions with Heliopolis, north-east of Cairo, the centre of this cult. If this were so we must consider that these kings were of the Anzety-folk, who seem to have been sun-worshippers. During the reign of his successor, Neneter or Neterimu, according to one interpretation of the Palermo stele, the first temple of hewn stone was erected, but of this no remains have been found. A more recent interpretation by Sethe attributes this temple to Khasekhemui, a king of the next dynasty. After the death of Sekhemab Perenmaat, the fourth king, the Set-folk of Upper Egypt revolted, and their chief, Perabsen, ascended the throne. The rightful monarch appears to have been absent in Nubia at this time, but in due course Khasekhem returned at the head of his troops and re-established the rule of the Falcon kings of the second dynasty.

The second dynasty came to an end about 3000 B.C. by the rise to power of this Khasekhem, an inhabitant of Memphis, who is considered by some as the last monarch of the second dynasty. On his accession he married Ne-maat-Hap, the heiress of the previous king, and assumed the name of Khasekhemui. After a reign of nineteen years he was buried at Abydos, near the tombs of the first dynasty kings, and in his grave was found the gold object, referred to in a previous chapter, which appears to have been of metal derived from Transylvania. This tomb chamber was built of squared blocks of limestone, the earliest stonework of the kind as yet found in Egypt.

His son Zoser, ' the holy ', who reigned for twenty-seven years, built the first pyramid, the famous step-pyramid of Sakkara. This was designed for him by Imhotep, his prime

Fig. 33. Slate palette of Narmer.

minister, architect, and physician, who was afterwards deified
as the patron of science, and as Imouthes identified by the
Greeks with Asclepius. The pyramid was enclosed by a wall
5,000 yards long by 3,000 yards wide, and through this en-
closure ran a double colonnade, 85 yards long, consisting of
forty-eight columns of white limestone, each over 3 feet in

FIG. 34.   Tomb of Khasekhemui, at Abydos.

diameter and about 16 feet in height, carved to represent a
bundle of reeds. This, the earliest stone temple yet discovered,
and one which has only recently been uncovered, shows that in
Egypt at this time architecture had already reached a high
stage. Zoser conquered some of the territory to the south of
the first cataract and set up a stele in the desert of Sinai, as did
Sa-nekht his brother and successor.

After the death of Sa-nekht there appears to have been a
period of unrest, and little is known of the subsequent monarchs

until the accession of Snefru, the last of the dynasty, or, as some think, the first king of the fourth dynasty. Snefru was a great organizer, and appointed governors over districts. He ruled with a firm hand the whole of the land from Lower

Fig. 35.   The pyramid of Zoser, at Sakkara.

Nubia to the sea, and kept at work a large number of miners in the mines of Sinai, whence he extracted copper ore, or, as some think, turquoise.   He erected two pyramids, one at Dashur and the other at Medûm.   A tomb, at one time believed to be his, has recently been found to the east of the great pyramid of Giza, the pyramid of Khufu or Cheops, who succeeded him and married Meritiotis his widow.   This tomb has now, moreover, been proved to be that of Hetepeth-eres, or Hetep-hers, daughter of the previous king, wife of Snefru and mother of Khufu.

Snefru died about 2900 B.C. and with him ended the third dynasty. It is thought by some that his immediate successor was Sharu, the Soris of Manetho's list. Only one monument of his has been found, and if he reigned it was but for a short

Fig. 36.   Pyramid attributed to Snefru at Medûm.

time, as his immediate successor Khufu married the widow of Snefru. Khufu, under the name of Cheops, is the best known of the early Egyptian kings, and the great pyramid which he built has long been reckoned one of the wonders of the world. It is indeed a marvellous feat of engineering, and the skill of its builders is such that though each side measured 755 feet, the

Fig. 37. The Great Pyramid of Khufu at Giza.

error is 'less than a ten-thousandth of the side in equality, in squareness and in level'. The stones are set together with joints of one-thousandth of an inch in thickness, involving edges and surfaces 'equal to opticians' work of the present day '.

Several volumes could be written on the pyramids, tombs, statues, and other works of Khufu and his successors Khafre and Menkaure. The period of the fourth dynasty was a time of prosperity, when gigantic works were undertaken with great skill. These are said to have been carried out by the disciples of Imhotep, the designer of the pyramid of Zoser. During the whole of this period the land was at peace, and most of the Pharaohs seem to have spent nearly all their time and energy in preparing stupendous tombs to hold their bodies after their death. Menkaure was succeeded by Shepseskaf, who died after a reign of at least four, or according to some eighteen, years. The name of his successor is unknown, for after a short reign of about two years he was deposed and the crown passed to a usurper from Heliopolis.

Userkaf, the usurper, ascended the throne as first monarch of the fifth dynasty about 2750 B.C. He was a nobleman of Heliopolis and high priest of Re, the sun-god of that city. A later legend states that he was the son of the god by Rud-dedit, the wife of Reuser, priest of Re. He seems to have been the first Pharaoh to have claimed divine origin if not actual divinity. From this time, too, we find a gradual increase in the importance of the worship of Re and in the influence of his priests. After a reign of seven years he died and was succeeded by his brother Sahure, who reigned for twelve, when a third brother, Neferirikere, whose personal name was Kakau, ascended the throne. Then followed three other kings, who are believed to have been sons of Kakau. These kings erected the pyramids at Abusir, between Sakkara and Giza, and it has been noted that in these the masonry is far from being of the fine type used in the fourth dynasty, as they were constructed round a core of rubble. Though the art of sculpture retained its high standard, it did not improve, and there are signs that degeneration was setting in.

FIG. 38. Restoration of the pyramids of Abusir and connecting buildings. (After Borchardt.)

During the reigns of these kings and of the three who followed them Egypt was peaceful and prosperous. The copper or turquoise mines at Sinai were worked to their full extent. Trading and exploring expeditions were carried out, both up the Nile and to the Red Sea, and by both routes to the land of Puenet, which seems to have been situated somewhere in Somaliland. Once, during the closing years of the dynasty, there was trouble on the north-east frontier, and some tribes from Palestine interfered with the operations at the mines.

A punitive expedition was undertaken, under the command of
Inti. The army attacked two villages, Nedya and En-Ka—,
took them by storm and massacred most of the inhabitants,

FIG. 39.   Life-size statue of the son of Pepi I.

carrying off the remainder as slaves. With the death of Unis,
about 2625 B.C., the fifth dynasty came to an end, and Teti
ascended the throne as first Pharaoh of the sixth dynasty.

It would appear that no violent revolution heralded the
advent of this dynasty, whose kings seem also to have been
priests of Re. Little is known of the first two Pharaohs, but

Fig. 40. A noble of the Old Kingdom hunting wild fowl.

the third, Pepi I, reigned for at least fifty years. A fine statue of him is in the Cairo Museum, made of copper, according to most authorities, though Mosso has declared it to be bronze with 6·557 per cent. of tin ; an analysis made quite recently shows that its composition is about 94½ per cent. copper, 3¼ silica, and that the balance is made up of traces of iron, nickel, and sulphur, but no tin. During his reign further attacks were made by the Heriu-Sha, ' those who are upon the sands ', who seem to have been inhabitants of southern Palestine. The command of a punitive expedition was entrusted to Uni, who assembled a large army from all parts of Egypt, including Libyans from the desert and negroes from the Sudan. Uni took part of his host by sea, perhaps as far as the north of Mount Carmel, so as to outflank his enemy, and then ' smote them all, and every insurgent among them was slain '. Pepi I was succeeded by his son Merenre Mehtimsaf I, who reigned three years and died at the age of sixteen. He was succeeded by his brother, Pepi II, who was six years old at the time and lived to be a hundred. During the early part of this reign Egypt flourished and was rich, but as the king aged his power declined and enemies appeared upon his borders and became increasingly menacing. After a reign of ninety-four years he was followed by Merenre Mehtimsaf II, who reigned for one year ; then in succession by Neterkere and Menkere, whose reigns covered only two years.

During the time of the fifth dynasty, and still more during that of the sixth, the power of the king, which had been paramount during the third and fourth dynasties, had been waning, and had passed in some measure to the great nobles, to whom had been entrusted the command of the punitive expeditions. During the last days of the long reign of Pepi II these became disaffected, and his successors were unable to control them.

DATE	DYNASTY	KINGS		DATE
B·C	VI	Teti		B·C
2700	V	Unis Ded Kere Isesi MenKauhor Neuserre An Khaneferre Neferefre Shepseskere Neferirikere KaKau Sahure User Kaf		2700
2800	IV	· · ✧ · · ✧ · · Shepses Kaf Menkaure Khafre Rededef Khufu Sharu ?	(Mycerinus) (Chephren) (Cheops)	2800
2900	III	Snefru Neferke Sanekht Zoser Khasekhemui		2900
3000	II	Senedi Peribsen Sekhemib Perenmaat Neneter Reneb Hotepsekhemui		3000
3100				3100
3200	I	Ka Sen Semerkhet Enezib Merpeba Den Za Zer Aha·Men Narmer	(Semti) (Abti) (Menes)	3200
3300				3300
3400				3400

Fig. 41 Chart of the Kings of the Old Kingdom of Egypt

Note. The chart reads, in order of time, from the bottom upwards.

After the death of the last king of the sixth dynasty, about 2475 B.C., these nobles struggled among themselves for the supremacy, and the chaos that followed left the kingdom a prey to outside invaders, the negroes from the south and the hill tribes of the Judaean plateau from the north-east. These overran the country, and history is almost silent for several centuries.

Such is, in brief outline, the history of Egypt from the unification of the kingdom until the fall of the Old Kingdom. We must now consider the progress of civilization, the life of the people, and their religious beliefs.

We have seen reason to believe that the most civilized element in the population of Egypt during predynastic times was that group, centred at Buto in the Delta, which had been responsible for the introduction of agriculture and many other arts. They came, we believe, from North Syria, and were partly, if not mainly, of Anatolian origin. During the later phases of the predynastic period they had been driven southwards by their western neighbours, who ruled from Sais. Then Narmer or Menes, leading the Horus worshippers from This, conquered the Delta and brought the whole land under his dominion.

There is no reason for believing that the people of This had a specially high civilization, in fact Peet has suggested that the Horus cult and the falcon emblem were borrowed from the tribe occupying Behdet in the Delta, though there are difficulties in adopting this view. It seems probable, however, that they were a virile body of men, civilized enough to appreciate the higher culture of their new subjects and prepared to learn from them.

The second dynasty, we have suggested, may have been founded by these wheat-growers, and from this time on we find among the ruling class the presence of a type of head and face strongly reminiscent of the type now found in Anatolia, a type that Elliot Smith has described as the Armenoid or Giza people. Few remains dating from the second dynasty have yet been found, but it is significant that Egyptian tradition attributes to a Pharaoh, who reigned at the close of this dynasty, the erection of the first stone-built temple, that is to say the first real advance in architecture.

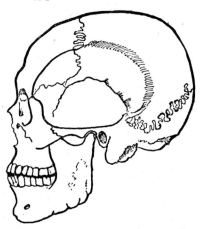

Stone building was at this time kept exclusively for tombs and temples, and most of the latter were adjuncts to royal and other important tombs. The predynastic Egyptians had buried their dead in a plain pit, covered with a heap of sand, around which was

Fig. 42. Profile of a skull from the Giza necropolis showing Armenoid traits.

placed a row of stones. During the first and second dynasties the pit was enlarged and lined with sun-dried bricks. The grave was still covered with a heap of sand, surrounded now with a brick wall. With Khasekhemui, the first king of the third dynasty, we find the brick wall of the pit giving way to a wall of ashlar limestone, and soon afterwards this develops into an underground chamber, covered by a sand heap, which is surrounded and covered by ashlar masonry. This type of tomb has been called a Mastaba. Soon after 2980 B.C. Zoser, as we have seen, erected a terraced tomb or pyramid, which in form represents a number of tombs of the preceding type, of dimin-

ishing size, placed one on the top of the other. Later, about
2930 B.C., a tomb like the last was erected by Snefru, but the
spaces between the terraces were filled with masonry in one slope,
so as to form a pyramid 214 feet high. The first true pyramid
was built by the same Pharaoh, a few years later, about 2900 B.C.
Khufu began the great pyramid at Giza, which has a height of 481
feet. Thus in about 150 years the royal tombs developed from
a plain stone-lined pit to the greatest and finest of the pyramids.

Of the evolution of temple architecture it is not so easy to
speak, for the earliest building of the kind that we know is that
in front of the terraced pyramid of Zoser. This has only
recently been uncovered and details have not yet been published. Judging by the preliminary descriptions that have
appeared, describing its fine columns carved to represent
bundles of reeds, it must have had many predecessors. Most of
the temples of this date that are known were attached to
pyramids and tombs, yet we have hints that other temples were
in existence. The principle of the arch had been discovered at
this time, though it was rarely used. It has been thought by
some that the art of working in stone was introduced by the
kings of the third dynasty, who were intruders and brought the
art from elsewhere. With this we cannot agree. Khasekhemui
seems to have been an inhabitant of Memphis, even if of
northern origin. In spite of the absence of direct evidence, the
deductions drawn from the perfection of Zoser's temple, and
the native tradition already mentioned, lead us to believe that
the kings of the second dynasty, who were, we are inclined to
think, of the Armenoid or Giza type, had introduced the custom
of building temples, and perhaps tombs also, in ashlar masonry.
Whether they were the first to discover this art, while endeavouring to copy in stone the bricks they had used for long,
or whether the art was introduced from the north-east, from

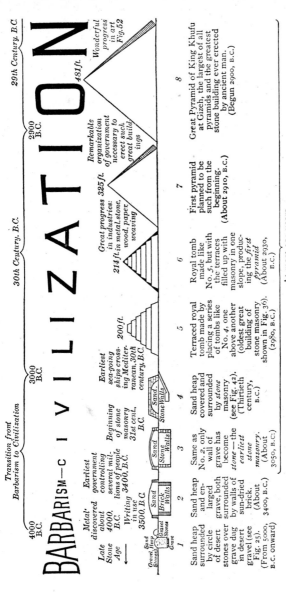

BARBARISM—c i v i l i z a t i o n

Late Stone Age

Metal discovered about 4000, B.C.

Earliest government controlling several millions of people Writing 3500. B.C.

Beginning of stone masonry 31st cent., B.C.

Earliest sea-going ships crossing Mediterranean, 30th century, B.C.

200 ft.

214 ft. Great progress 325 ft. in industries: in metal, stone, wood, paper weaving

481 ft. Remarkable organization of government necessary to erect such great buildings

2900 B.C.

Wonderful progress in art Fig. 52

Gravel Heap. Sand Gravel Stones Grave

1

Sand heap surrounded by circle of desert stones over grave dug in desert gravel (see Fig. 25). (From 5000, B.C. onward)

Sand | Brick Walls

2

Sand heap and enlarged grave, both surrounded by walls of sun-dried brick. (About 3400, B.C.)

Sand | Stone Walls

3

Same as No. 2, only wall of grave has become *stone*—the *earliest stone masonry.* (About 3050, B.C.)

Sand | Stone Walls

4

Sand heap covered and surrounded by *stone* masonry (see Fig. 42). (Thirtieth century, B.C.)

5

Terraced royal tomb made by placing a series of tombs like No. 4, one above another (oldest great building of stone masonry shown in Fig. 36). (2980, B.C.)

6

Royal tomb made like No. 5, but with the terraces filled up with masonry in one slope, producing the *first pyramid* (About 2930, B.C.)

7

First pyramid planned to be such from the beginning. (About 2910, B.C.)

8

Great Pyramid of King Khufu at Gizeh, the largest of all pyramids and the greatest stone building ever erected by ancient man. (Begun 2900, B.C.)

At most 150 years (from earliest stone masonry to the Great Pyramid).

FIG. 43: Diagram showing the evolution of the Egyptian tomb from the sand-heap to the pyramid.

a land where soft stone was present but clay for brick-making was lacking, cannot yet be determined.

Dwelling-houses throughout this period were made of clay or bricks ; even the royal palaces were never constructed of

Fig. 44.   Third dynasty arch, from a tomb at Bet Khallaf.

stone. The king lived in a brick-and-mud house with a double gate, which signified the double kingdom ; before this flew standards from poles of cedar brought from Lebanon. Around the palace were the houses of the nobility, of similar though perhaps more simple type. The mass of the people lived crowded in humble dwellings in mean streets.

FIG. 45.   Villa and garden of an Egyptian noble of the Old Kingdom.
(After Perrot and Chipiez.)

The use of stone bowls, first introduced from the Arabian Desert at the beginning of the middle predynastic period, continued throughout the time of the Old Kingdom, and fresh forms were introduced and the workmanship carried to a high pitch of perfection. The use of such stone bowls became so common that the quality of the pottery declined, though it began to improve again during the fourth dynasty. It has

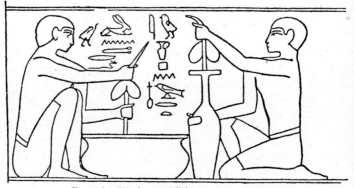

Fig. 46. Workmen drilling out stone vessels.

been stated that the potter's wheel was introduced early in this dynasty, but it has been asserted by others that wheel-turned pots occur, though rarely, in first dynasty tombs. Whence it was introduced is uncertain.

Copper implements became commoner and of more varied form as civilization improved, and it is just possible that the secret of alloying copper with tin or some other metal had been discovered before the close of this period. We have already referred to the fine statue of Pepi I, found at Hieraconpolis and now in the Cairo Museum. It has been stated that this is made of an alloy containing nearly 7 per cent. of tin, but this statement has been proved to be inaccurate as the result of a fresh analysis. A bronze rod, said to date from the fourth dynasty, was found by Petrie at Medûm, but this at present stands alone, and it is thought by some that it had fallen in from a higher layer during the progress of the excavations. It is to be hoped that full analyses will soon be made and published of all the metal objects known to date from the time of the Old Kingdom.

We have seen that in early predynastic times boats, made of bundles of reeds, were used on the Nile, and had become com-

Fig. 47. Metalworkers' workshop in the Old Kingdom.

mon in the middle predynastic period. At the same time there is reason for suspecting a sea traffic between the Delta and Syria, though possibly in foreign ships. The evidence from Crete also leads us to suspect maritime intercourse before the times of Menes. Large river-craft were in use during the first and second dynasties, and towards the close of the third Snefru dispatched forty ships to the Phoenician coast to bring back large baulks of cedar from Lebanon. During the fifth dynasty Sahure sent a naval expedition down the Red Sea, and an illustration of one of these ships appears on the walls of the temple of his pyramid at Abusir.

The early Badarian invaders of Egypt have left small ivory

statuettes, and the art of carving in this substance and in soft stone progressed throughout the predynastic period, though there was no serious attempt at portraiture until its close. The portrayal of the features with accuracy was attempted when it became of importance to place in the tomb the figure of the dead man, for he would stand a better chance of living in the underworld if the statue buried with him were a true likeness. It was, however, sufficient for this purpose that the face should

FIG. 48.   Representation of a sea-going ship, found among the wall reliefs in the pyramid temple of Sahure.

be lifelike ; the accuracy of the trunk and limbs was unimportant. This attempt at portraiture seems to have begun during the second dynasty, and the earliest figure that we know bears the names of the three first kings of that dynasty. Two seated figures are known of Khasekhem, whom we have identified with Khasekhemui, the first king of the third dynasty. Later portrait-statues become commoner and reach their zenith during the fourth dynasty, when statues both in diorite and wood, of kings, queens, and nobles, attain a lifelike perfection never subsequently reached. The effect of religious influences during the fifth dynasty was to formalize the art, which became still more stereotyped during the sixth.

We have already spoken of the tombs, and we must now say

a word about the funeral customs, which formed such a striking feature in Egyptian custom and belief. The preservation after death of the body was the great desire of the Egyptians, as it was believed that some kind of life remained as long as the body was intact. Much care was lavished on the tombs, to which offerings of food were taken at regular intervals. The rich soon lined their tombs with sun-dried brick, to add to the comfort of the departed, while the poor were content with a simple pit, covered with a mat, which soon became silted up with sand.

FIG. 49. Granite statue No. 1, Memphis.

Now this sand was impregnated with *natron* or soda, so that the bodies in the graves became pickled while those in the brick vaults gradually decayed. In due course this difference was discovered and its cause determined. Instead, however, of abandoning brick vaults for graves, the rich experimented in methods of pickling the corpses of their relatives in solutions of *natron*. Thus by slow degrees arose the custom of mummification. The first clear evidence that we have of the custom, still in its initial stages, is in some of the tombs of the second dynasty. It was not, however, very successful, and the use of portrait-statues was to act as a substitute for the corpse should the latter decay. The practice had become more successful during the fifth and still more during the sixth dynasty, which may, perhaps, account

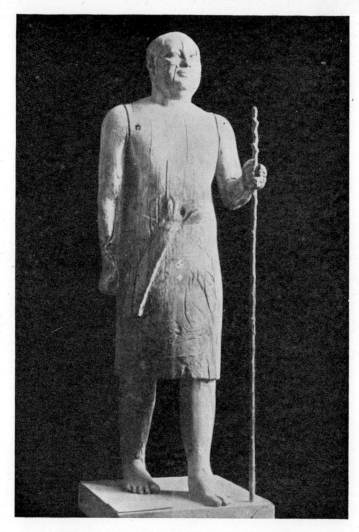

FIG. 50. Wooden statue of the Sheikh el-Beled.

in part for the decline in the art of portraiture. It was still only adopted by royal personages and a few great nobles, nor was the custom general until quite late in Egyptian history.

We have seen that the Egyptians were deeply concerned with what happened to their bodies after death, believing that continued existence depended on the preservation of the body or,

FIG. 51.   Body of a woman from a predynastic burial in Egypt.

Reproduced, by kind permission, from the collections in the Field Museum of Natural History, Chicago.

at a later time, on the presence in the tomb of a lifelike statue, which the *ka* or soul could occupy. This was their first crude notion of an after-life, which was the cardinal feature of their religion. The earliest temples seem to have been erected at the tombs of kings and later at those of great nobles ; many of the priests were but attendants at these temples, engaged to see that the material, and perhaps spiritual, wants of the deceased were attended to.

Other priests there were, but these seem rather to have been noble laymen who acted in this capacity, a position reminding us somewhat of the patesis in the Sumerian cities. Each city or village, as in Sumer, had its own patron deity, and a sign or crest, usually in the form of an animal, which was displayed in early days on a banner. As the country became unified these

Fig. 52. Head of King Khafre.

deities became associated, each presiding over special activities and each represented by a human figure with the head of the heraldic beast of his city. Thus Thoth, the Ibis-headed god, originally of a village in the north-east of the Delta, became the god of letters, and took to himself all the legends of the moon. By degrees, however, these local gods were combined

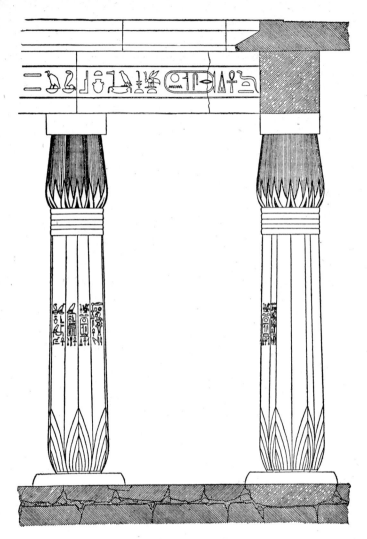

FIG. 53.   Elevation of part of the colonnade surrounding the court of the pyramid temple of Nuserre (fifth dynasty).

into a system ; they were treated as members of one family, each with his special function, and an elaborate theological system was raised on this basis.

A priesthood as a special class began to arise during the fifth dynasty. The *Uer-maa* or Great Seer of Heliopolis was

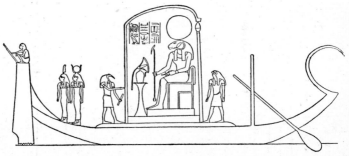

Fig. 54. The celestial barque of the sun-god, with other deities on board.

a noble more priestly than lay, and the same was true of the two high priests of Ptah in Memphis, who both bore the title of *Uer-khorphemtiu* or Great Chief of Artificers. As time went on the priests became more a class apart from the laity, though they were never a distinct caste as Herodotus has suggested. Later on their power became greater and weak monarchs were often much under their influence.

BOOKS

BREASTED, J. H. *A History of Egypt* (New York, 1912).
HALL, H. R. *The Ancient History of the Near East* (London, 1913).
PETRIE, Sir W. M. FLINDERS, *A History of Egypt*, vol. i (London, 1923).
SMITH, G. ELLIOT. *The Ancient Egyptians* (London, 1911).
The Cambridge Ancient History, vol. i (Cambridge, 1923).

5

Early Minoan Times

Hitherto we have been watching civilization developing in the great valleys of the Nile and Mesopotamia, where people could pass readily by the margin of the river or up and down stream in light craft. This ease of communication led early to the foundation of cities and ultimately to the formation of extensive kingdoms. In the Aegean world geographical conditions were different. This relatively small sea is filled with islands of various sizes, packed so closely that none is out of sight of some other on fine days. The mainland on either side is mountainous, with short valleys leading in one direction to difficult passes, in the other to seaports capable of harbouring small ships. This led to the formation of a vast number of small communities, which could readily communicate with one another by sea, when boats of sufficient sea-worthiness had been built, while it made the foundation of large kingdoms difficult.

To the south of this region lay the long narrow island of Crete, connected at either end by chains of islands with Greece and Asia Minor ; although exceedingly mountainous, it is penetrated by at least two good passes from north to south. Owing to its size and to the richness of certain plains near both shores Crete obtained the rudiments of civilization earlier than other parts of the Aegean world ; more than this, the relative nearness of Egypt, 400 miles away it is true, brought it into touch with the more advanced culture of the Nile before this could reach territories farther north.

In the last part we pointed out that the presence in Crete and elsewhere of obsidian from Melos and of other foreign objects implied that navigation was not unknown, and after

3093·4   G

3400 B.C. we find positive evidence of sea-going ships. The simultaneous development of civilization both in and around the Aegean Sea, which, as we shall see, begins about this time, seems to indicate that voyages were now undertaken with greater frequency and, we may imagine, with fewer risks.

When reviewing the results of his wonderful discoveries at Knossos, Sir Arthur Evans noted that the culture was continuous from the time that metal first appeared until the destruction of the Bronze Age civilization by invaders with swords of iron. This continuous culture he termed Minoan,

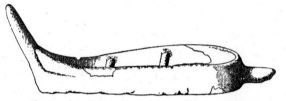

FIG. 55.   Clay model of a boat of the Second Early Minoan period.

from Minos, the legendary king of Crete. He noticed, too, that there were three well-marked periods in which Minoan culture had reached a high stage, and that each of these had been preceded by a period in which the art was ruder but progressive, while each was followed by a time of decline. For this reason he divided the whole of the Minoan epoch into three greater periods, which he termed Early, Middle, and Late Minoan, and each of these again into lesser sub-periods of advance, acme, and decline, which he distinguished as I, II, and III. Some of these at a later time he still further divided into two sections, A and B. Thus we have nine sub-periods, some of them still further subdivided, ranging from Early Minoan I to Late Minoan III.

We have seen in the previous part that the neolithic inhabitants of Crete had traded with Egypt, taking thither obsidian from Melos and perhaps emery from Naxos. In return they had brought back stone bowls of predynastic type. At the beginning of the Early Minoan period we find a sudden advance in the civilization of the island. There is not only abundant evidence of trade relations with Egypt, but we note the introduction of customs that had arisen in the Nile valley. We find the use of palettes, such as were used in Egypt from early predynastic times, amulets in the forms of legs and monkeys and of figures that are thought to represent mummies ; besides these there are copper tweezers of Egyptian form and other objects that seem to hint at the arrival of settlers from North Africa. These have been found more commonly on the plain of Mesara, on the south of the island.

This has led Evans to make the important suggestion that these new elements of culture were due to the arrival of refugees from Egypt, Tehenu from the western Delta, who fled to Crete about 3400 B.C. when Menes conquered their country. We have seen reason to believe that the Tehenu had cultivated the olive on the western edge of the Delta. The facts that in Crete the olive was cultivated in Early Minoan times and that before the close of the period, as we shall see in a later part, they were in the habit of exporting their surplus oil to the valley of the Nile, give additional support to this suggestion. About the same time we find in the tombs the presence of a small proportion of broad skulls ; as these have been found for the most part in the east of the island and as the skulls are of a type common to-day in Anatolia, we cannot be wrong in assuming that these broad-headed intruders had come from Asia Minor. There is also evidence that about this time some people from the Cyclades settled near Mochlos.

Since objects, closely resembling those made in Egypt during

the fourth and subsequent dynasties, have been found in deposits of Early Minoan II date, it is thought that this sub-period

Fig. 56.   Amulets, which are thought to represent mummies.   *a*, from
Egypt ;   *b*, from Hagia Triada, Crete.

coincides with these dynasties.   In the lower half of the deposits
at Knossos attributed to Early Minoan I no metal objects had
been found until recently, and Evans had termed these layers
sub-neolithic, or, as we should prefer to say, epi-neolithic.   We

could not assume, however, that during this time metal was wholly unknown, but that it was scarce, at any rate in the northern part of the island. In fact a copper axe-head has recently been found by Evans in a house of this period. It seems likely that such metal objects as existed were imported from Egypt, and that the Cretans had not yet discovered the copper deposits in the east of the island nor learnt how to smelt the ore, though copper was used in the east earlier than in the centre of the island.

We may therefore adopt the following chronological system, feeling confident that it is not far from the exact truth:

Early Minoan II ⎰ B.   2600–2400 B.C.
                     ⎱ A.   2800–2600 B.C.

Early Minoan I ⎰ B.   3100–2800 B.C.
                 ⎱ A. Epi-neolithic   3400–3100 B.C.

It appears probable, as we have seen, that the neolithic inhabitants of Crete kept domesticated animals, at any rate during the latter part of that period. The remains that have come down to us from the First and Second Early Minoan periods throw no fresh light on the subject. Neither have we any fresh evidence as to the cultivation of grain, though the fact that during this time the greater part of the population was concentrated on the lower and less rocky lands, especially on the plain of Mesara on the south, suggests that agriculture had begun. If Evans is right in bringing the new-comers from the Delta, it can hardly have been otherwise, though the Tehenu seem to have been more addicted to pastoral than to agricultural pursuits ; we have seen reason, too, for believing that they now cultivated the olive. They lived, in all probability, largely on fish, flesh, and dairy produce, though it is likely that grain was grown, if only to a small extent. They seem also to have known how to spin and weave, though evidence of this is scanty and not very conclusive.

Their houses, as in late neolithic days, were small rectangular structures built of dry stone, though towards the end of the first period some of these became larger, and in the second period they are often of considerable size with many rooms. There are cases in which the houses had two or even three stories, though the upper stories were built of brick. Their bricks were large

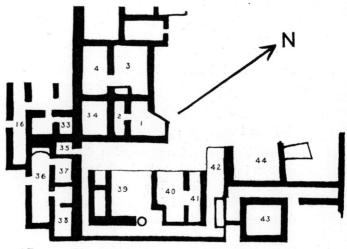

FIG. 57. Plan of Early Minoan II buildings at Vasiliki (Seager).

and sun-dried and were set in a framework of wood. The whole interior was sometimes plastered with lime, and painted with a red wash. Certain models found at Phaestos suggest that round houses were sometimes built.

The pottery of this period is very varied in form and decoration. During epi-neolithic times many of the old neolithic types survived but they disappeared before the advent of Early Minoan I b., when painted pots, which had already come into use, entirely superseded them. All the pots were made without a wheel, of reddish clay, frequently covered with a red slip, though later this gave way to buff. The decoration, especially in Early Minoan II, was geometric, and the designs were in dark lustrous paint on a light background. Similar pots have been found at Syros in the Cyclades. Other wares were grey,

FIG. 58. Pottery of the First Early Minoan period.

while some, shaped like chalices, with grained decoration, were clearly copied from wooden models.

Axes and knives of stone and obsidian continued in use throughout the period, but from Early Minoan I B onwards copper tools became increasingly common. Copper knives and triangular daggers occur in Early Minoan I B, copper cutters, like flat axes but hafted like chisels, are not uncommon, and by Early Minoan II B the daggers had become elongated and somewhat ogival in form, while the perforated axe-adze, used earlier in Mesopotamia, had reached the east of the island. So numerous are the copper objects of this date in the island that we cannot doubt that the Cretans had discovered the deposits of copper ore in the east of the island. The existence of ' house-tombs ' near Gournia, dating from the Second Early Minoan period, seems to show us that the veins of copper ore, which gave rise

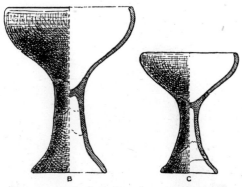

FIG. 59. Grained chalices on a wooden model.

to a flourishing bronze industry at that place in Middle Minoan times, had already been discovered and worked.

Objects of gold have been found in considerable quantities, dating especially from Early Minoan II ; the most notable examples of the goldsmith's art are the articles of jewellery, dating from this time, found in a tomb at Mochlos. Silver was relatively scarce, though a pair of silver daggers have been found, which seem to date from the closing phase of this period. Whence the Cretans obtained their gold is uncertain, for there are no deposits on the island, though the metal was at a later date found near Sardes in Asia Minor. It is well, however, to remember the fragments of gold in the tomb of Khasekhemui, which are thought to have come from Transylvania. If they came from so distant a source they may well have been taken to Egypt by Cretan mariners.

Dr. Xanthoudides has explored a large number of tombs around the plain of Mesara, which date from this period. These are circular buildings of dry stone walling, gradually diminishing in size, by means of corbelling, as they ascend. He concludes

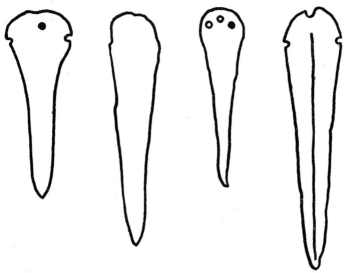

Fig. 60. Copper daggers from Crete.

that they terminated at the top with a small aperture closed by a large capstone. The objects found in these tombs are of very different dates and show that most of them were erected in the First Early Minoan period, while all remained in use until First Middle Minoan times. Vast quantities of human bones were found in each, showing that they must have contained hundreds, perhaps thousands, of bodies. The conclusion is that they were family or tribal vaults, in use for a great many generations, and

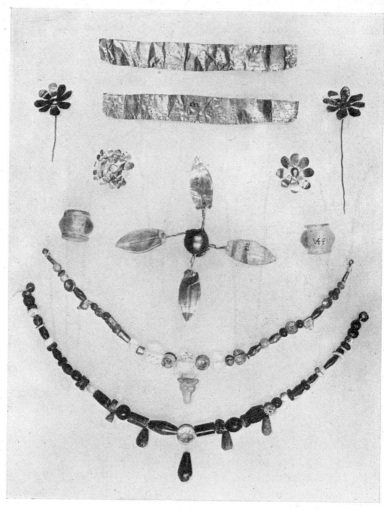

FIG. 61. The treasure of Mochlos.

that each time fresh bodies were placed in them the remains of the earlier burials were disturbed. Inside the tombs there was evidence that fires had been lit, for many of the bones were charred and the stonework was begrimed with smoke. It is clear, however, that the bodies were not cremated, and it has been suggested that the fires had been lit to purify the atmosphere.

FIG. 62. The tholos of Kalathiana.

The doorways leading into these beehive tombs, or *tholoi* as they are called, are relatively low, and the jambs often consist of two upright stones on which rested a large stone as a lintel ; this was often humped or gabled in the centre to relieve the superincumbent weight. The doorways were often closed with a large stone slab. These doorways open out into small pits or yards, with walls about six feet in height ; these sometimes contain bones swept out of the tombs, but may also have held offerings to the departed. How these yards were entered is not clear, as no opening has been found ; it is conjectured that the bodies were lifted over the wall and that the bearers climbed over it by means of stone steps or ladders. There is some evidence that earth and stones were heaped up around the tombs to the height of about six feet, so that only the upper part of the *tholos* would have been visible.

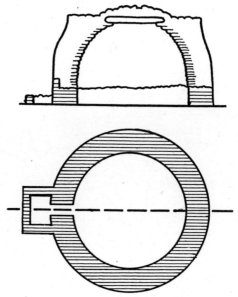

Fig. 63.   Diagrammatic plan and section of a tholos.

It is thought that these tombs were built to imitate houses, but the foundations of Cretan houses of this period so far found are always rectangular, though models of round huts have been found at Phaestos. Xanthoudides has pointed out that on the plain of Nida on Mount Ida in the centre of the island there are some cheese dairies still surviving which are built exactly on the same model. He adds, too, that on the top of Mount Ida there is a little chapel dedicated to the Holy Cross built in precisely the same way without mortar.

Evans has suggested that the circular beehive tombs were introduced at the beginning of the Early Minoan period by the invaders from the Delta, and has pointed out that huts of this form have a wide distribution in North Africa, especially in Libya, just west of the Delta, whence he would bring these

Fig. 64.   Modern cheese dairy on Mount Ida.

folk. Other types of graves are sometimes found, some rectangular like the Cretan houses, roofed with clay and reeds, and some in caves or rock-shelters. In the east of the island have been found stone cists, made of upright slabs of stone ; these, which show Cycladic influence, date only from the close of the period we are discussing.

Of the religion of the early Cretans we know little, but we have evidence that as early as Early Minoan I they worshipped the Great Mother, their chief deity of later times. This goddess seems to have been a concept very similar to that of Cybele, worshipped in Asia Minor, and we shall find traces of like beliefs elsewhere in the Mediterranean region. Figures of this goddess were not often made, though representations of her occur on seals. She is more often represented as a pillar or a holy tree. Among other cult objects we find the so-called ' horns of consecration ', which we meet with in Early Minoan I, the *pectunculus* shell, which is found even in neolithic deposits, and the

Fig. 65.   The Great Mother and horns of consecration.   From a sealing.

double-axe, a symbol from Asia Minor, which appears somewhat later. There is nothing to tell us whether they had an order of priests to lead their worship; but if we may judge from the evidence of later times, a priestly caste was an idea foreign to the Cretans, who, like the Sumerians of old, had an officer who combined the functions of priest and king.

We have seen that the Cretans took sea voyages even in neolithic times ; models of boats from Early Minoan graves give us some idea of their craft. That they traded with the Cyclades, Cyprus, and Egypt, even from very early days, has already been made abundantly clear, but there are indications that during the times with which we are now dealing their commercial relations covered a still wider field.

A carinated bowl with two handles, found in a cave at Miamu,

FIG. 66. Vases from the cave at Miamu.

resembles some found at Troy, while a square-mouthed carinated vase from the same site bears a close likeness to some found in a neolithic deposit in some Ligurian grottoes. Whether the Cretans had reached the Western Mediterranean at so early a date is uncertain, but it seems likely that they had at any rate indirect connexion with some Italian centres about this time.

BOOKS

CHILDE, V. GORDON. *The Dawn of European Civilization* (London, 1925).
EVANS, A. *The Palace of Minos at Knossos, Crete*, vol. i (London, 1921).
GLOTZ, G. *The Aegean Civilization* (London, 1925).
The Cambridge Ancient History, vol. i (Cambridge, 1923).
XANTHOUDIDES, S. *The Vaulted Tombs of Mesara* (Liverpool, 1924).

The Aegean World

FOR practical purposes we may divide the Aegean world at this time into six regions, though of five only of these have we any certain evidence at present. The island of Crete, the largest in the area, we have already discussed. The others, of which the group known as the Cyclades has been the best studied, form another well-marked region, the civilization of which is called Cycladic.

The mainland on the European side falls into two not very clearly marked regions, Greece proper, the ancient Hellas, the culture of which is known as Helladic, and the great plain of Thessaly, within its ring of mountains, where there existed a totally different type of civilization, which we know as Thessalian. During the earlier phases Central Greece, lying between Thessaly and the Peloponnese, falls rather into the Thessalian region, though later, in the Second Thessalian period, it becomes more and more influenced by Helladic culture, which occupies the whole of this area before the close of the Early Minoan period.

The coastal areas of Asia Minor fall into two distinct regions. The northern part, which includes the mound of Hissarlik, the site of the famous city of Troy, we may call the Phrygian region, while the southern part, known later as Caria, the early remains of which are little known, we may term the Carian region.

Those who have investigated the early civilization of the islands, consider that this can be divided into nine sub-periods, contemporary with those of Crete ; these have been named in the same way, ranging from Early Cycladic I to Late Cycladic III. Lastly, much more recently, the same system was

Fig. 67.

applied to the mainland of Greece, where the sub-periods range from Early Helladic I to Late Helladic III.

Most students of Greek archaeology consider that these three sets of periods and sub-periods are contemporary, that Early

Minoan I and Early Cycladic I cover the same period of time as
Early Helladic I, and that the same is true for Late Minoan III
and Late Cycladic III. Professor Glotz has, however, recently
suggested that this is not absolutely so, for the earlier of the
Helladic sub-periods should be placed, he thinks, at a somewhat
later date than the others. Thus he considers that Early Helladic I is contemporary with Early Minoan I and II, Early
Helladic II with Early Minoan III and so on, though he admits
that Late Helladic I and Late Minoan I are contemporary. It
appears to us, however, that there is at present insufficient evidence to support this readjustment, and we prefer to follow the
more orthodox system of chronology. We admit, however,
that there is little evidence for the existence of Early Cycladic I,
and that during the First Early Helladic sub-period the culture
in Greece was Thessalian.

We have seen that during neolithic times obsidian from Melos
reached Crete, and emery, probably from Naxos, was used in
Egypt, where also a bowl of marble from Paros was found in a
tomb of the first dynasty. No evidence, however, has been
found on the spot that can be earlier than the beginning of the
Metal Age. Our evidence for the First and Second Early
Cycladic sub-periods is confined to tombs and their contents ;
but these give us some idea of the pottery of the time, as well
as of the tools, jewellery, and artistic productions.

We have no means of ascertaining whether the early inhabitants of the Cyclades cultivated grain or possessed domesticated
animals ; though, since they had long been trading with Egypt,
they cannot have been entirely ignorant of either. No houses
dating from this time have been found, so nothing is known of
their domestic architecture. The pottery was rough hand-made
ware of a mud-coloured clay, ornamented with incised designs,
usually in straight lines. There is little difference to be noted

DATE	CRETE	ISLANDS	HELLAS	THESSALY	HISSARLIK	DATE
2500	EARLY MINOAN II B	EARLY CYCLADIC II	EARLY HELLADIC II	THESSALIAN II	HISSARLIK II	2500
2600						2600
2700	EARLY MINOAN II A		EARLY HELLADIC I	THESSALIAN I	HISSARLIK I	2700
2800		EARLY CYCLADIC I				2800
2900	EARLY MINOAN I B		(Thessalian)			2900
3000						3000
3100						3100
3200	EARLY MINOAN I A (Epi-neolithic)					3200
3300						3300

Fig. 68 Chart of the early civilisations of the Aegean Region

Note. The chart reads, in order of time, from the bottom upwards.

between the pottery of the two First Early Cycladic phases ; in fact some authorities state that no pottery has been found that can be attributed with certainty to the first phase.

There can be little doubt that metal was known to the Cycladic folk as early as to the Cretans; but, as they had a mono-

poly of obsidian, which they exported widely, it is likely that they did not encourage the spread of metal implements which competed with their trade ; copper ore, however, exists in Paros, Seriphos, and Siphnos. Few implements of metal have been found that can safely be dated before the Third Early Cycladic phase, and these probably came in by trade. Among the numerous orna-

FIG. 69. Incised vase of Early Cycladic II.

ments buried with the dead were beads, rings, and pins. Diadems, not unlike those found at Mochlos in Crete, were not uncommon, but were of silver, not of gold. Though the latter metal was not unknown, silver was more commonly used, while the reverse is the case in Crete.

The tombs are of various types. Plain quadrangular cists of stone slabs are not uncommon, though in Syros the more usual type was a small polygonal vault of dry masonry, diminishing as it ascended by means of corbelling, and covered with a capstone. These were entered through a doorway which led out of a small porch or courtyard. In Euboea have been found chamber-tombs cut in the rock and approached through a stepped pit. These, however, may be a little later in date. *Tholoi*, like those in Crete, did not come into use until the Third Early Cycladic phase. The graves usually contained single interments, though several bodies were sometimes deposited in the same tomb ; this, however, seems to have occurred only in the case of poor people, if we may judge from the quality of the grave-goods. Family or tribal vaults, like those found in Crete, are quite unknown.

Of the religion of the Cycladic folk we know little, but vast numbers of small figures, usually in marble, have been found, which are believed to represent the Great Mother. This cult we have found also in Crete, together with figures that seem to have been of Cycladic origin. It has been suggested that both regions derived this cult from Asia Minor.

It is clear from what has been already said that the Cycladic folk were great traders. They took obsidian, marble, and emery to many lands, and brought back gold, silver, copper, and lead, though in time they found the two last metals in their own region. It has been thought that they reached the northern edge of the Aegean and even penetrated to the plain of South Russia. Objects of Cycladic type have been found in both these areas, but it is uncertain whether they date from so early a time. Various articles, which remind us of this culture, have been

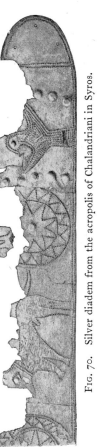

FIG. 70. Silver diadem from the acropolis of Chalandriani in Syros.

found also farther west—in Sicily, Italy, and beyond; these may indicate later movements. At the beginning of the Early Cycladic period the people of these islands made considerable settlements on the north-east shore of Crete, and it may be that it was Cycladic masters who paved the way for the great expansion of Cretan trade.

The mainland of Greece seems to have been settled at a

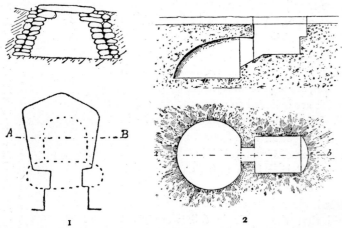

FIG. 71. Cycladic tombs. 1, Syros ; 2, Euboea.

relatively late date by a few intruders from the northern region, for the first evidence that we possess, which is very scanty, shows us a people, still ignorant of metal, but using pottery very similar to that made in the Thessalian region, which we shall describe later. This culture is fairly generally distributed in Central Greece, at Chaeronea, Orchomenos, and Hagia Marina. Later traces of it have been found at Korakou near Corinth, and in Arcadia and Argolis. The rest of the Peloponnesus seems to have been uninhabited.

FIG. 72. Figure of the Great Mother.

At the beginning of the Third Early Cycladic phase, that is to say about 2800 B.C., the inhabitants of the Cyclades made settlements on the southern shores of the Peloponnese,

FIG. 73.   Pottery of Early Helladic type.

especially in Argolis at Tiryns, Mycenae, and Asine ; later on they crossed the pass and settled on many sites around Corinth. Later still they crossed the Gulf to Thisbe and made their way to Boeotia. No further advance was made, however, until the Third Early Helladic period. Very little has been found that dates from this time, but the pottery was for the most part a dark-faced burnished ware, with a red, brown, or black surface, often decorated with incised patterns. The pots were ovoid in form and seem to have been copied from leather vessels.

All the evidence available suggests that the people responsible for the Early Cycladic and Early Helladic cultures were intru-

FIG. 74. Early Helladic pot.

ders, and we must inquire whence they came. In spite of some resemblances, due probably to the interchange of products in the course of trade, the Cycladic culture differs considerably from that of Crete. As we shall see later, it bears no resemblance to those found in the Thessalian and Phrygian regions, while it intrudes late into the Helladic. Though no positive evidence yet exists, the Carian region seems to be the most probable source of this culture, for there are complete chains of islands, never as much as twenty miles apart, linking the Cyclades with this part of Asia Minor. Though many graves have been discovered, only one skull has been found and described ; this, which came from Antiparos, is somewhat broad-headed, having a cranial index of 80·9. This and the fact that Cycladic graves appear in the north-east of Crete during the First Early Minoan period, when broad skulls make their appearance at the eastern end of the island, suggests that people from the Carian region of Asia Minor began to investigate the resources of the islands at an early date, to settle there in considerable numbers about 3400 B.C., to colonize Eastern Crete at the same time, and about 2800 B.C. to form settlements in Argolis.

The Thessalian plain, which is in reality two plains separated by a range of low mountains, was inhabited at an early date, though whence the people came is a mystery. The plains are surrounded on all sides by high mountains, and access from the sea can be obtained only over two low passes in the south-east or through the narrow gorge of Tempe in the north-east. The western half of the western plain, at the foot of Mount Pindus, was densely wooded and remained uninhabited until much later.

The earliest pottery found here is polished red ware of a very fine type. It has thus been described by Mr. Forsdyke : ' This is hand made, but thin, and is fired very hard and bright. Notwithstanding the absence of metal in the Thessalian settlements, and the abundance of stone implements, it is evident that some of the forms of this pottery were derived from metal prototypes.' That the people who first occupied Thessaly, and who seem to have had no metal, could have evolved such a type of pottery on the spot is impossible, and we must consider whence they came and where they developed the potter's art.

This neolithic culture of Thessaly, known as Thessalian I,

has nothing in common with the civilization of Crete or the Cyclades, and was in fact ousted from the Peloponnese by the latter. Its stone implements somewhat resemble those found in the Danube basin, but the pottery is quite distinct ; also metal was only known in the Danube valley to a limited extent until

Fig. 75.   Pot of Thessalian red ware from Tsangli.

much later and, as we have seen, the Thessalian pottery was originally copied from metal models. Vessels not unlike this red ware have been found in the Vardar valley, but overlying black-faced fabrics, which are more nearly allied to the pottery of the Second Thessalian period. Only two sites in the Phrygian region have been fully explored, Hissarlik and Yortan, and at neither of these sites have wares been found resembling this red ware, though some of the vases from Yortan may possibly have been derived from ancestral forms common to them and Thessalian ware. It seems clear, then, that this culture could not have reached Thessaly either from the north-east or from the north-west.

Professor J. L. Myres has written much about a type of red ware which succeeded black wares at Hissarlik and elsewhere. He tells us that ' the region over which it seems to be at home extends from Palestine on the south, to the Hellespont westward, and to the Upper Euphrates, or possibly further east '. If the Thessalian red ware is, as seems likely, an offshoot of this Anatolian red ware, it can scarcely have come round the north of the Aegean, past Yortan and Hissarlik, where the forms are so different and where the red ware did not appear until the close of Thessalian I. Nor could it have passed through Thrace and Macedonia, where it is absent but for late examples. It must, we think, have been brought across the Aegean Sea, past Chios, Psyra, Scyros, Halonnesos, Peparethos, and Sciathos to the Pagasatic Gulf, whence two low passes would admit the invaders into the two plains of Thessaly. If this explanation is correct, red ware, ancestral to that of Thessaly, should be found in some of these islands and in the neighbourhood of Ephesus on the mainland of Asia Minor, and farther inland in the direction of Pisidia, where other examples have been found.

The people with this red ware seem to have been the first inhabitants of the mainland of Greece, and may, perhaps, have been reinforced by some of the folk from the Danube basin ; this, however, is not likely, as no Danubian pottery, attributable to this date, has been found in Thessaly, while the resemblances between the stone implements of the two regions, which are not very close, may be accounted for if both cultures derive ultimately from a common source in Asia Minor. The red ware

FIG. 76. Pots from Tsangli.

people seem first to have settled in the Thessalian plains and the valleys of the Spercheios and Cephissus just to the south ; later on they spread still farther south, across the isthmus to the neighbourhood of Corinth and even into Arcadia beyond. When they came is uncertain ; some authorities suggest as early a date as 3500 B.C., while others would be content with 3000 B.C.

The discovery of carbonized grain in some of their settlements shows us that the First Thessalian folk cultivated the land, while the presence in their refuse heaps of the bones of oxen, sheep, and swine proves that they kept domesticated animals. Since, however, the bones of deer were also found, we must assume that they had not altogether abandoned a hunting life. At first they built for themselves round huts of crude brick, but before the end of the period they erected in their villages rectangular houses of brick on stone foundations.

At first their pots were plain, or decorated with incised lines or a series of stamped points ; after a time the potters added simple linear ornaments in white paint. Later the surface was covered with a white slip, on which rectilinear decoration was added in glossy red paint. In the south the plain red ware was replaced by a thin black ware ornamented with knobs.

Metal seems to have been unknown to these people ; they had knives of obsidian, apparently derived by trade from Melos, and stone celts or hoes, among which is a type, not unlike that found in the Danube basin, known as the shoe-last celt. They wore shell bracelets and perhaps necklaces of clay beads, though these may perhaps be spindle-whorls ; if this be so, it is clear that spinning and weaving were known.

No burials of this period have been found, so we have no direct evidence of the racial affinities of these people, and little on which to form an opinion as to their religious beliefs. Some

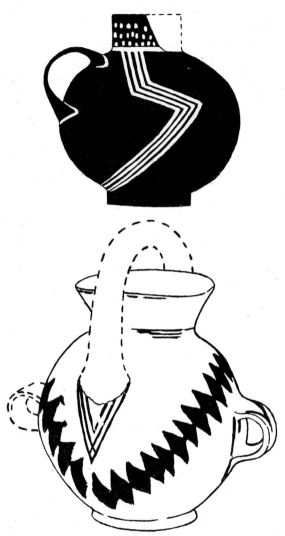

FIG. 77. Painted pots of Thessalian I from Tsangli.

statuettes of fat women, clasping their breasts with their hands, are thought to be images of the Great Mother, a further indication that their original home was somewhere in Asia Minor.

Our knowledge of the life of these people is scanty; they

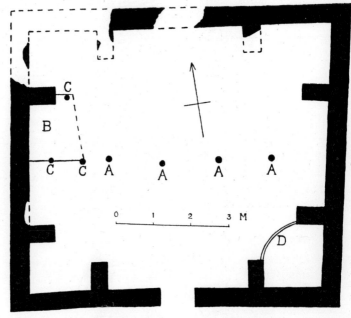

FIG. 78. Plan of House T at Tsangli.

seem to have been peaceful growers of grain, with a few domesticated animals, living in villages, without metal. They held little communication with their neighbours, except that they sometimes bartered their spare products with Cycladic mariners who brought them obsidian from Melos. The quantity of refuse found on the sites of their villages seems to indicate that they dwelt in Thessaly for many centuries with little change of custom, until at a date variously estimated at 2500 or 2600 B.C., of which we prefer the latter, fresh intruders from the north made themselves masters of the land. Who these were and

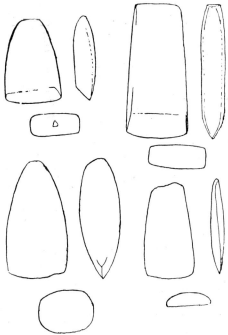

Fig. 79. Thessalian celts. After Tsountas.

whence they came are questions which must be left to be discussed in the next part.

Every one has heard of the heroic excavations carried out by Schliemann at the mound of Hissarlik, near the Dardanelles, in search of Priam's Troy. Less known, but more valuable for our purpose, are the subsequent explorations made later by his assistant Dörpfeld on what was left untouched by his master. The result of the later examination was to ascertain that a number of settlements had been made successively on the site of Troy, and that the second of these, the third or burnt city of Schliemann, had been twice rebuilt. It was found, too, that after a succession of later villages, known collectively as His-

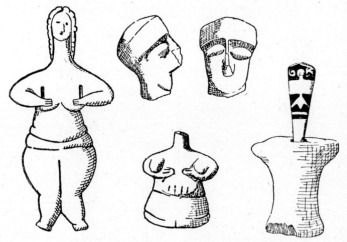

FIG. 80. Thessalian figurines. After Wace and Thompson.

sarlik III, IV, and V, had disappeared, there arose the sixth city, whose destruction by the Achaeans is the subject of Homer's *Iliad*.

The second city is usually thought to have been built about 2400 B.C., and its foundation cannot be placed later than the beginning of the Third Early Minoan period. It may well have existed earlier, for, though no remains of Early Minoan II or Early Cycladic II have been found in its ruins, the first settlement is believed to have been contemporary with Early

FIG. 81. Troy as it appeared after the excavations of 1879.

Minoan I. The civilization of Hissarlik II has much in common with that of Thessalian II, as will be seen when we come to describe both in a later part. We are inclined, therefore, to date its foundation about 2600 B.C., or perhaps rather earlier. The village known as Hissarlik I will, therefore, be roughly contemporary with Thessalian I, or with the later stages of that culture.

This unpretentious village consisted of rectangular houses

FIG. 82.   Jugs from the first settlement at Hissarlik.

with walls of crude brick on stone foundations, which remind us of the later dwellings of Thessalian I ; they were enclosed by a ring wall. The pottery was hand-made and black with a polished surface, sometimes ornamented with simple linear designs in thin white paint. The inhabitants were acquainted with copper, though the metal was scarce. Stone celts were common. Whether these people grew grain is uncertain ; but they kept cattle, sheep, pigs, and goats, and lived to a great extent on fish.

Two divisions of this period can be distinguished ; but the site seems to have been abandoned some little time before the foundation of the second city, which we believe to have taken place about or just before 2600 B.C. It seems likely that the first settlement was made about 3000 B.C. or possibly a little earlier.

BOOKS

CHILDE, V. GORDON. *The Dawn of European Civilization* (London, 1925).
GLOTZ, G. *The Aegean Civilization* (London, 1925).
SCHLIEMANN, H. *Ilios* (English translation) (London, 1880).
The Cambridge Ancient History, vol. i (Cambridge, 1923).
WACE and THOMPSON. *Prehistoric Thessaly* (Cambridge, 1912).

7

The North Kurgan at Anau

WE have described in a previous part the two mounds or kurgans at Anau in Turkestan discovered by Pumpelly and excavated by him with the assistance of Schmidt. We there showed that the North Kurgan was the older of the two and that it arose from the accumulation of the debris of long-continued occupation. We suggested that this occupation probably lasted from about 3900 to 2750 B.C., though there is still considerable divergence of opinion as to these dates, and no evidence has been forthcoming so far which will enable us to fix them with any degree of certainty.

Although the civilization portrayed by the relics found in the North Kurgan is continuous, Schmidt has divided the time during which it was occupied into two periods, known as Anau I and Anau II. The first of these we described in the last part, and here we have only to point out the changes that are apparent during the period known as Anau II, which we have dated provisionally as having lasted from 3300 B.C. to 2700 B.C.

As was the case during the first period the houses were rectangular and built of air-dried bricks ; no kiln-burnt bricks were as yet in use. A new feature, however, was the use of

Fig. 83.   Pivotal door-stone of house.

door-slabs of stone set with pivotal hinges ; we find also ovens shaped like the upper half of a pot. The custom of burying their children beneath the floor in a contracted position continued throughout this period. Wheat and barley were still grown, and the long-horned ox, the pig, horse, and two breeds of sheep, known in the first period, were still kept. During the second period, however, there were added to their stock a short-horned ox, a breed of hornless sheep, the goat, the camel, and the dog. These additions have been thought to betoken the arrival of a new people, or at any rate new elements of culture from the east. If new people arrived they were apparently few

FIG. 84. Pottery from Anau II.

in number or else closely allied to the earlier inhabitants, for the second civilization is clearly a continuation of the first. It seems more likely that in these new elements we should see only trade relations with the east.

There was but little change in the style of the pottery. It

was still hand-made and sometimes painted with geometric decoration ; but during the second period a monochrome ware, either red or grey, was more commonly used.

Tools were still to a great extent made of flint, and the only fresh type found in the deposits of the second period was a

Fig. 85.   Pot from Anau II.

flint sickle. As in the earlier period there is a singular lack of implements that could have been used for hunting or fighting, though in the second period sling stones first appear.

Copper and lead were known during the first period, though both metals were exceedingly scarce. During the second period both of these become commoner, especially the former, and copper pins are by no means rare. Fragments of a copper torque were found, and a blade that might have belonged to a spear-head or a dagger.

Turquoise beads were known to the inhabitants during the first period, but during the second, though these remained in use, the people had the choice also of beads of carnelian and lapis lazuli.

It will be seen from the foregoing very brief description of this second period at Anau that there was very little change in the civilization of the people, who were busy cultivating their fields and seem to have had little intercourse with their neighbours, except, perhaps, on the east.

At a date which we have fixed provisionally at 2750 B.C., though it may well have been a century or two later, the village was abandoned. Whether the climate became drier and the streams that irrigated their fields dried up, as some have suggested, we have no means of telling. Such was the fate of very similar settlements in the Khotan at a very much later date, as Stein has shown us. Perhaps the nomad cattle men of the Northern Steppe destroyed the village and put its inhabitants to death. All we know

FIG. 86. Dagger blade from Anau II.

is that the village came to an end and was not refounded on the same site.

BOOKS

PUMPELLY, R. *Explorations in Turkestan* (Washington, 1905–8).

8

The Peasants of the Danube Basin

In Chapter VI we saw that a people, who cultivated the land, lived in villages and made pottery, were occupying the plain of Thessaly about 3000 B.C. or perhaps earlier. We have now to describe a population that was occupying parts of the Danube basin at about the same time. Their civilization, which in many respects resembled that of Thessaly, is known as Danubian ; the stage that we shall now describe is known as the First Danubian period or Danubian I.

The Danube rises in the plateau of South-west Germany and most of its tributaries drain the mountain areas of Central Europe. Its basin may for convenience be divided into three sections. The Upper Danube basin contains Bavaria, Austria, and the eastern half of the Alpine ranges. The Middle Danube basin lies mainly between the Carpathians and these Alpine mountains ; in the midst of this lies the great plain of Hungary. The Lower Danube basin, which is narrow, extends between the gorge through the Carpathians, known as the Iron Gate, and the Black Sea. All the evidence we now possess of the First Danubian civilization comes from the Middle Danube basin or just outside its borders.

The Hungarian plain is usually described as an extension of the Steppe-land of South Russia ; this, however, is scarcely accurate. Much of the soil is loess, it is true, but loess of a somewhat heavy type, which during periods of fairly heavy rainfall would have borne woodland, even if not of a very dense type. Over large areas the soil is alluvial, especially in the neighbourhood of the rivers. This alluvial soil must once have

MAP OF THE DANUBE BASIN

Note—Mines represented thus ⊙ Gold □ Copper △ Tin + Cinnabar

Fig. 87.

been marsh, subject to constant flooding, and, as it became drier, would have become densely wooded, as much of it is to-day. Across the northern part of the plain, in the latitude of Buda-Pest, the soil is sandy, and this sandy area was formerly more extensive. Persistent west winds, however, blowing down the Upper Danube Valley, caused the sand to set itself in parallel ridges, each lying from north to south. Between these ridges marsh conditions arose under a wetter climate, and these, now drier, are covered with dense woods ; the sandy ridges, however, are open or sparsely covered with beech trees.

While some of the earliest villages that we are now to describe lie in the plain, on raised patches of loess near the rivers, the majority lie on the outskirts, between the mountain and the plain, between the forest and the steppe or swamp. These settlements fall naturally into two groups, in which, although the chief items of civilization are almost identical, certain well-marked local differences appear. These groups lie mainly in the north-west and south-east of the Middle Danube basin.

Into the north-west corner of the Hungarian plain opens the broad valley of the March, which joins the Danube about twenty-five miles below Vienna. Higher up, the March valley opens between the Sudetes and the Beshkids through a broad low pass into the loess zone of Poland. The basin of the March forms the province of Moravia, once a part of the kingdom of Bohemia and now the centrally placed province of the Czecho-Slovakian Republic. The pass is known as the Moravian Gate, and through it have passed many invaders from the north and east, while it also formed one of the ways through which Christianity and Latin culture passed from the south into Poland.

All the earliest sites of the northern group of First Danubian settlements so far discovered lie in Moravia, though during the second half of the period this civilization had spread north-westwards into Bohemia and north-eastwards through the Moravian Gate into Silesia. The evidence derived from the sites shows us that the people who had developed this civilization lived in villages of irregular oval huts, sunk some little way into the ground and situated near the streams on patches of sandy loess. In these have been found querns for grinding corn and shoe-last celts, somewhat resembling those of the Thessalians,

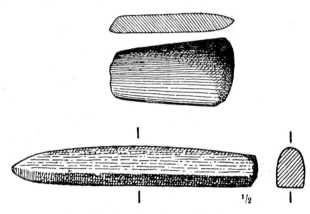

Fig. 88. Shoe-last celts. After Seger.

which were the heads of hoes ; these show us that the inhabitants cultivated grain.

The people had a number of domesticated animals including short-horned cattle, the marsh sheep, and the pig. Bones of long-horned cattle, *Bos primigenius*, have been found in their settlements, but these may have belonged to wild animals hunted and killed for food. The evidence available suggests, however, that hunting was not practised habitually, for the remains of game are scarce, and are rarer still in the later settlements. No spears, arrows, or other sporting implements have been found, and the only weapons hitherto discovered on these sites are disk-shaped mace-heads of stone.

The earliest pottery found in these Moravian villages is very well made and is clearly not a first attempt ; the potter's art must have been known to its makers for a long time. It is slate grey in colour and the surface has been carefully smoothed. The shapes are many but all of them suggest the gourd, which is a plant not native to Europe, though it grows wild in Asia Minor and Syria. The pots have no regular handles, but some of them are furnished with knobs or lugs. The bowls and bottles are usually ornamented with very distinct decoration. Designs are engraved with shallow incisions, sometimes varied with small pits. The patterns always consist of pairs of parallel lines, whence this ware is frequently called ribbon ware, a translation of the German name *Bandkeramik*. These bands or ribbons often take the form of spirals or meanders, whence the term, now coming into general use, spiral-meander ware.

Female figurines or idols of baked clay have been found in some of the settlements, though these are rare ; they are very crudely modelled. They are thought to represent the Great Mother, a cult that is believed to have had its original home in Asia Minor. The most remarkable feature of this civilization, however, is the presence of bracelets made from the shell of *Spondylus gaederopus*, a mollusc that inhabits the Mediterranean Sea. These are found on all the sites of the First Danubian period, and should throw some light on the original home of this civilization or its trade relations with other countries.

Very few burials of this date have been met with, and it is not clear that those discovered belong to the people responsible for this civilization. A few isolated graves have been found in Lower Austria, Moravia, and Bohemia, where the dead have been buried in a contracted position. The skeletons show us a people of short stature with moderately long heads. Some think that these resemble the people of the Mediterranean lands, whom we have called Southern Steppe-folk; but Schliz, who has made a close study of the remains, says that they differ in important respects from the Mediterranean skulls, and classes this people as a branch of the Nordic race, which we have termed the Northern Steppe-folk. It may be, as some have suggested, that the Danubian folk burned their dead and that

Fig. 89.   Spiral-meander ware.

these burials are those of intruders from the loess regions of Poland or the sand-dune areas in North Hungary.

About the middle of the period a new type of pottery makes its appearance in Moravia. The ware itself is very similar to the earlier type, but the shape of the pots and their decoration are quite different. These later pots are of a form known as carinated. The lower part has the form of a wide shallow bowl at the rim of which the curve changes from convex to concave, leaving a sharply defined 'keel', from which its name is derived. This shape, which we shall meet with elsewhere under very different conditions, seems to have been derived from a leather model.

When considering a somewhat similar type from the first
settlement at Susa, Frankfort suggested that the leather prototype was made thus. A circular piece of leather was beaten out
until it assumed the shape of a saucer or shallow bowl, then a
cylinder, formed, perhaps, of several strips sewn together, was
fastened to the rim of the bowl. The sides of the cylinder would
fall in when the bag was placed on the ground and thus assume
the carinated form shown in Fig. 90. That this type of pot is
derived from a leather model is further shown by the decoration,

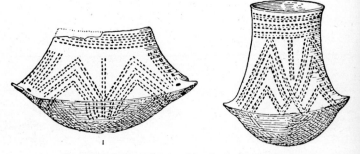

FIG. 90.   Carinated pots of stroke-ornamented ware.

which consists of parallel lines made up of a series of fine strokes or
wedge-shaped impressions, reminiscent of stitching, and, perhaps,
of cords for suspension before the upper portion was added. These
impressions were sometimes filled in with white paste.

From the nature of its decoration this pottery is called
stroke-ornamented ware. It is first met with in the upper
layers of the settlements in Moravia, where the other elements
of the First Danubian civilization remain unchanged. About
the same time villages with spiral-meander pottery were established in Bohemia to the north-west and in Silesia beyond the
Moravian Gate.

The appearance of a new type of pottery suggests the arrival of a new people ; the fact that the earlier type seems to spread at the same time to the north-west and the north-east suggests that the new-comers arrived from the south. The leather form of the pottery leads us to suspect that the makers were either hunters or nomad pastoral tribes, and these inferences suggest to us that they came from the plain of Hungary. On the other hand Childe is of opinion that these people lived in Galicia and Silesia, and that the early Danubians first came into contact with them after they had spread through the Moravian Gate. Direct evidence, however, of the existence of such people in the sand-dune area on the north of the Hungarian Plain has just come to light, for remains of a culture, resembling the Tardenoisian, have recently been reported from Áldozó (Co. Śzolnok), Hugyaj (Co. Szabolcs), and Koronczo (Co. Gÿor).

We must now turn to the southern group of sites. Most of our information comes from a village site at Vinča, near Belgrade, where the stratified remains of several periods have been found. Here we find oval huts, sunk in the ground, shoe-last celts, rude clay idols and bracelets of *Spondylus* shell as in Moravia. Moreover, though the shapes of the pots differ somewhat from the Moravian type, they are decorated with ribbon patterns and, in all but the lowest layer, with spirals and meanders.

The forms of the vessels do not resemble those of gourds, but we find pedestalled bowls, and urns with a human face on the rim and with lids, which remind us of some found in the second settlement at Hissarlik, which we shall describe in our next part. A few of the vases have a red slip and have been thought to resemble some from Hissarlik II, but they are more like the red pots of the first period in Thessaly. Another ware, decorated by scratching off part of a sooty slip, reminds us of pots from Boz Euyuk in Phrygia and others of a rather later date from Thessaly. A very few small copper beads have been found in the settlement and a number of flat bone harpoons. North of Vinča, by the banks of the Theiss and other rivers, are several similar settlements.

On the east the river Maros enters the Hungarian plain from the Transylvanian mountains, and some little way up its valley, beyond the frontiers of Transylvania, lies Tordos, where another village settlement has been found containing remains very closely resembling those of Vinča. Pedestalled bowls and urns with lids and faces occur here too. Tordos, in spite of some local peculiarities, clearly belongs to the southern group of early Danubian settlements, though a few painted pots found here show us that its inhabitants had come into contact with some neighbours, who will be described in the next chapter.

We have now set out all the essential facts and we must endeavour to interpret them. We must first inquire during what centuries the people responsible for this civilization occupied the Danube basin. The shoe-last celts and bracelets of shell remind us of the First Thessalian culture, as indeed does the red pottery from Vinča. The pedestalled bowls and pots with lids and faces occur in the second period at Hissarlik, but beyond these no further resemblances occur, while other objects, much more like those from Hissarlik II, arrive in the Second Danubian period. The first civilization of Thessaly was brought to an end by invaders who introduced, among other things, porched houses and concentric fortifications, which will be described in our next part. The second city at Hissarlik also has porched houses, though the fortifications, built of brick, have only a single line of defence. In the Second Danubian civilization, as we shall see, we have many intrusive elements which resemble those found in the second city of Hissarlik, while at Lengyel in Hungary is a concentric fort very closely resembling the second Thessalian fort at Dhimini ; this has been thought by some to date from the Second Danubian period, though others would place it later. The inference is that the foreign influences which brought to an end the First

Fig. 91. Pedestalled bowls from Vinča.

Danubian period were the same as those which led to the building of the second city at Hissarlik and were contemporary with the second civilization of Thessaly.

The face-urns, however, do not seem to belong to the invading people who founded Hissarlik II, but are rather of native manufacture. Very similar designs, though on handles of jugs, occur with pedestalled bowls, as we have seen in Chapter III, in the cemetery A at Kish, which dates from about 3000 B.C. if not earlier. The motive seems to have been derived from the south-east, and may well have reached Vinča some time before the foundation of Hissarlik II.

Though there must still remain some uncertainties as to dates, all the evidence points to the view that the First Danu-

bian period came to an end about 2600 B.C. or perhaps a little later. When it began is still more uncertain. Some authorities have suggested that its beginnings must be dated as early as 3500 B.C., but as the depths of the deposits in Moravia are not great, we prefer the more modest estimate of 3000 B.C., though the villages in the southern area, where the deposits are deeper, may well have been founded earlier.

Lastly, we have the still more important problem to solve : whence came these people and their civili-

FIG. 92. Face-urn from Hissarlik.

zation ? It seems unlikely that the potter's art started independently in the Danube basin, especially since the earliest specimens that we possess are not the work of beginners. The art cannot have been derived from their neighbours to the north or west, who were still living in epi-palaeolithic darkness, nor does the pottery resemble that of the Danish shell-mounds, which may well be of later date. If it is unlikely that the potter's art sprang up independently in this region, it is still more unlikely that the cultivation of grain did so, for it is extremely unlikely that any such plants as wheat or barley grew wild in Central Europe.

We have already seen occasion to indicate resemblances between this civilization and that of the First Thessalian period ; also to note the differences. The gourd-like form of the earliest Moravian wares seems to indicate an eastern origin, for plants of the gourd family are native to Palestine and Asia Minor, but not, it is believed, to Europe. The resemblances, faint as they are, between the face-urns of Vinča and Tordos on the one hand and Hissarlik and the distant Kish on the other seem to indicate a line of approach.

We have seen reason to suspect that the early Thessalian civilization came, perhaps from Pisidia, across Anatolia and the central islands of the Aegean Sea. We would suggest that the Danubian civilization passed by a similar but more northerly course from a not far distant region. This would account for. the resemblances between the two cultures which we have already noted. Crossing the great plain that lies in the centre of Anatolia, or perhaps skirting the northern foot-hills of the mountains that lie between Iconium and Sardes, they would reach the Aegean Sea, perhaps at Smyrna, or more probably at the mouth of the Caicus. It is possible that they took a more northerly route and crossed the Hellespont ; if so it would be tempting to think of them as passing up the valley of the Maritza and down the Nishava-Morava to Vinča. These valleys are, however, narrow and well wooded, and search for remains of this civilization has been made in vain between Belgrade and Nish. Childe has suggested that they were experienced sailors and reached all parts of the Danube basin by boat. In support of this view he mentions that all the sites hitherto discovered lie on the banks of navigable rivers and streams. This view, if accepted, will accord well with the suggestion made above that they reached the Aegean Sea at or near the mouth of the Caicus. It must not be forgotten, however, that other causes, such as the need of an adequate water-supply, or the custom of moving along the banks of rivers, might equally lead to riverside settlements, and it is possible that the Hellespont route was taken and that the intruders travelled along the shore of the Black Sea and along the northern foot-hills of the Balkan mountains. It is true that no evidence of their presence in Bulgaria has come to light; on the other hand, this region has been little explored.

If our Danubian peasants came from Anatolia we should expect them to be broad-headed like the bulk of the population of that region then and now. Yet the few graves that have been found have yielded skulls which are moderately long. At first sight this seems to lessen the value of our suggestion. It has been pointed out, however, by Myres and others that the early round-headed populations of Central Europe seem to have burnt their dead, and, if this was the case, the burials so far found will be those of foreigners, no doubt received into Danubian communities and using Danubian pottery, but retaining their own burial customs. The paucity of the graves found in comparison with the number of villages excavated makes this explanation all the more probable.

We have seen that during the middle of the First Danubian period there appeared in Moravia, from the south as we believe, a new type of pottery, derived, we have thought, from leather models. We have already suggested that the leather prototypes may have been used by hunting or pastoral tribes on the Hungarian plain. Judging by what we know of the distribution of early man in Europe we should expect this plain, the sandy portions of which may be considered as an outlier of the Northern Steppe, to have been peopled by those whom we have designated the Northern Steppe-folk, among whom there had mingled, to judge from the distribution of microlithic implements, some elements of the Southern Steppe-folk, who had entered Europe as Final Capsian invaders. Some of those who have examined the skulls claim that they are of Mediterranean type, while Schliz maintains that they are Nordic. If they are the skulls of this hunting folk, who were a mixed people inhabiting, as we believe, the western sections, at any rate, of the

FIG. 93.   Gourd-shaped vessels of the First Danubian period.
After J. L. Pič.

Northern Steppe, we can readily understand this difference of opinion.

Lastly, a word must be said about the ubiquitous presence of bracelets made from the shells of *Spondylus gaederopus*. Mr. G. C. Robson informs us that this mollusc is found not only in the Mediterranean proper but also in the Aegean Sea. It would seem that it has not yet been recorded from the Sea of Marmora or the Black Sea, but the records of the Molluscan *fauna* of these seas are few and probably imperfect. If, as we have suggested, these Danubian peasants moved slowly across Asia Minor and perhaps the Hellespont, they would have touched the northern Aegean and might well have met with these shells on their way.

Childe has suggested that they were men of Mediterranean type who wandered from Palestine or Syria round the coasts of Asia Minor. Apart from the difficulties of this coastal route, where steep mountains often extend to the sea-shore, we think it unlikely that they could have come this way without picking up some elements of Cycladic and more elements of Thessalian culture.

The gourd grows wild in Anatolia as well as Syria, but it is not native to Europe ; yet the people of Moravia made their pots after the form of gourds, while those at Vinča and the neighbouring settlements did not. This appears at first sight anomalous. Some writers decline to see any close resemblance between gourds and the Moravian pots, and maintain that the forms of the latter are natural to early potters. With this we cannot agree. We are inclined rather to approve a recent suggestion of Childe's that the early intruders into the Danube basin brought with them gourd seeds and grew these plants at Vinča, for the gourd will ripen there though not in Moravia. It was only when the Danubians had passed far to the north that they were unable to produce dry gourds for vessels and so took to imitating them in clay.

We have already noted that no metal has been found in the First Danubian settlements in Moravia, though copper beads have come to light at Vinča. Metal objects are rare in these southern settlements, but the copper beads mentioned do not stand alone. It is a strange fact, and it cannot altogether be a coincidence, that the largest settlements in the southern area are close to metal deposits. Not far from Vinca is a cinnabar mine. Tordos is in the very centre of a region where lie the richest deposits of gold now worked in Europe, deposits whence much precious metal was obtained during the time of the Roman Empire. Near other sites there are copper mines. It is probable that the First Danubian people, when first they entered the Danube basin, were well acquainted with metal and knew how to work it, though it would appear that the colonists who wandered to the north-west soon lost that knowledge. It would seem likely that the gold found in the tomb of Khasek-hemui, king of Egypt, to which reference has already been made in Chapters I and IV, came from the Maros valley and from near Tordos, so that it is clear that gold was being mined in Transylvania at a date which cannot be later than 3000 B.C., the date that we have accepted for the Egyptian monarch. If our Danubians were good sailors, as Childe has suggested, they would have had no difficulty in carrying this commodity to Crete, if not to Egypt itself.

BOOKS

CHILDE, V. GORDON. *The Dawn of European Civilization* (London, 1925).

9

The Valley of the Alt

WE now come to one of the last civilizations that we have to describe here, perhaps the earliest civilization on the mainland of Europe ; this is certainly the last to be discovered, the least known, and the most mysterious. It has been called, from the place where it was first discovered, the civilization of Erösd.

In the extreme east of Transylvania, lying just within the

eastern arc of the Carpathian mountains, is the valley of the
Alt, sometimes called the Aluta or the Olt. The Alt rises in
the north, in the county of Čsik, then runs due south to the
neighbourhood of the town formerly known as Kronstadt and
now as Brasov or Brasso. Here it bends sharply to the north-
west, then turns to the south-east, after which it passes southwards through the Transylvanian Alps, crossing the Wallachian
plain to join the Danube.

Near the source of the Alt is the copper-mine of Balanbanya.
Charles Boner, who visited these parts in the early sixties of
the last century, says that near Balan it was customary to place
old iron spoons and pans in the bed of the river, which is here
a babbling brook. After a time these became coated with
a deposit of pure copper, which was then scraped off and sent
to the furnace. As we have seen, gold is found in abundance
in Transylvania and was mined there by the Romans. The
gipsies still wash the sands of many of the streams for the
precious metal, but whether it has been found in the bed of the
Alt or of any of its tributaries is uncertain. A tributary, which
joins the Alt just before it passes through the Transylvanian
Alps, rises close to the Maros, in the bed of which gold has been
found in abundance.

About the year 1910 the late Dr. Ferencz Laszlo, Curator of
the museum at Brasso, began exploring in that neighbourhood.
Near Erösd, a few miles north of Brasso, he discovered and
excavated several sites, and later he found one after another
along the higher reaches of the Alt and its tributary, until they
totalled twenty-two. At Erösd, the type site, there were the
remains of three superimposed settlements, which he has described very carefully, while the other sites were in all cases
contemporary with these though the stratification was not so
clear.

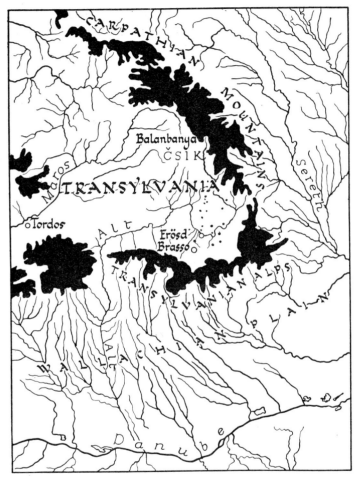

Fig. 94. Map of the basin of the Alt.

The earliest village at Erösd was a very small settlement, containing in Laszlo's opinion about twenty-one houses. It was situated on a spur of the hills, two sides of which were nearly precipitous, while the third was defended by a deep ditch and rampart ; it was, in fact, a typical promontory fort. Whether the defensive work belongs to the earliest settlement is uncertain. The houses of the first village were very small pit-dwellings, sunk some feet into the ground, leaving the earthen sides somewhat overhanging.

The occupants had shoe-last celts, sometimes fitted into ' sleeves ' of perforated deer antler to lessen the jar caused by

FIG. 95.   Clay stamp or pintadera.

a blow. These ' sleeves ' occur in Thessaly, at any rate in the second period, and appear later in Switzerland. These celts or hoes indicate here, as elsewhere, that the people of Erösd were cultivators of grain. They also kept domesticated animals, for numerous bones have been found among their refuse ; these have not yet been examined, but baked clay models of cattle, sheep, goats, and pigs have been found among the ruins.

Besides the celts the inhabitants of Erösd had rude flint implements, made of flint flakes, retouched on one side only. The most important remains, however, are their personal ornaments. They used clay stamps, known to archaeologists as *pintaderas*, for painting their bodies, as did the epi-palaeolithic hunters in many parts of Central Europe. These stamps bear some resemblance to the button seals found later in Crete,

Hissarlik, and elsewhere. They also used axe-shaped beads—marble beads in a neighbouring village—shell disks, bored teeth, and small pieces of bone perforated at both ends and apparently sewn on to their clothes.

More important, however, are the bracelets and spiral ornaments of copper wire found in the first and subsequent settlements, for this is one of the earliest sites at which metal has been found on the mainland of Europe. It is true that some copper

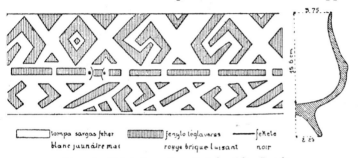

Lampo sargas fehér blanc jaunâtre mat   fenyло téglaveros rouge brique luisant   fekete noir

Fig. 96.   Painted cup from Erösd.   After Laszlo.

beads have been found at Vinča, but at Erösd there are copper ornaments in abundance, and copper ore exists, as we have seen, near the source of the river.

Finally, small ornaments of gold have been found in the earliest settlement. Whether the people of Erösd washed the sands of their river or of any of its tributaries for the precious metal is uncertain. No gold, it would seem, is sought for there at the present time. We have seen, however, that there is an easy pass from the Alt valley to that of the Maros, reaching the latter valley at that part of its course where gold is most abundant. Moreover, painted pottery, closely resembling that found at Erösd, has been discovered at the First Danubian station of Tordos, just a little lower down the Maros valley.

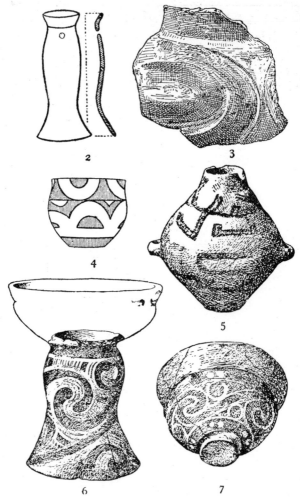

2   3

4

5

6   7

FIG. 97.   Pottery from the Alt valley.

The people of Erösd had evidently set up trade relations with the neighbouring valley; it is even possible that they had settlements there, or that some of them dwelt among the Danubian inhabitants of that region.

We must now turn to the pottery, the most distinctive product of the Erösd civilization. In the first settlement it is already well made, of distinctive form and decoration, and

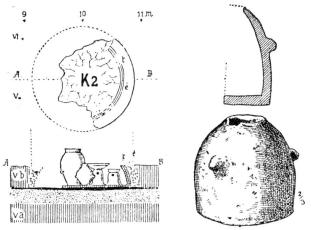

FIG. 98. Actual potter's oven and model found at Erösd. After Laszlo.

shows no sign of the models on which these were based. It is obviously not a new industry, and the first settlers must have arrived in the Alt valley when their potter's art had long passed its infancy. It shows no signs of development or degeneration, and the specimens from all three layers may be treated as identical.

The pots, made of fine clay, were well burnt to a red colour, and were painted in many styles, often in several colours. They were decorated with spirals and meanders, which, however,

take forms very different from those on the pots of the First
Danubian civilization. Some are modelled so as to bring this
decoration into relief; and the raised portions are further
emphasized by white paint.

The ovens used for baking these pots were circular and
domed, with an opening at the top. One of these was found by
Laszlo, as also the model of another.

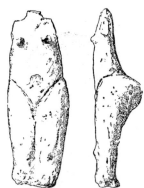

Fig. 99.   Clay figurines from
the Alt valley.

Lastly, many rude clay figurines
were found, mostly female and erect,
though some are seated and occasion-
ally, though rarely, male. A canoe,
made from the trunk of a tree, has
been found near Erösd, but it is not
clear that it dates from this period.
No graves have been found here.

As we have seen, it is not possible
to distinguish between the pottery
found in the three layers at Erösd.
A few slight differences, however,
have been noted in other details. In
the lowest layer the houses were all dug out of the ground and
were very small. In the second layer a porched house appears,
though it is not clear that this type was general. In the third
layer, or immediately on the top of it, have been found sherds
of another ware, roughly made, and decorated with impressions
of twisted cord. We shall come across other examples of this
cord or string ware in a later part; here it is sufficient to say
that it seems to be found first in a rather more northerly region.

There is reason to suspect that this civilization in the Alt
valley is contemporary with that in the Hungarian plain
and that it began before 3000 B.C.; its close seems marked by
the arrival in Thessaly of an almost identical civilization, which

reaches there about 2600 B.C., ushering in the Second Thessalian period. Whence it came it is more difficult to determine, but a very similar civilization has been found to the east, across the Carpathians. This we shall describe in the next chapter, where we shall deal also with the problem of the origin of both.

BOOKS

CHILDE, V. GORDON. *The Dawn of European Civilization* (London, 1925).

10

The Black Earth Lands

WE have seen in a previous part that a great grassy steppe stretches across South Russia from Turkestan to the foot-hills of the Carpathians, extending westwards across Galicia and the Wallachian plain. North of this lies a belt of park-land, with woods and clumps of trees interspersed with large open grassy areas and leading on with increasing density of trees to the forest lands around the upper reaches of the Volga. Throughout the open spaces in this park-land, and to some extent over the northern areas of the steppes, lie what are known as the Black Earth Lands, containing the richest agricultural land in Russia. The richness of this soil tempted cultivators of grain at an early date to settle in this area, which later became the granary of Ancient Greece and of Modern Europe.

Though the Black Earth Lands have not yet, except in Galicia, been explored archaeologically as thoroughly as most parts of Western Europe, a large number of sites have already been described; these have produced evidence of a very distinct type of civilization, beginning at an early date and lasting for many centuries. At a few sites two distinct periods can be distinguished. This is especially true for Cucuteni in Roumania, where Dr. Hubert Schmidt records two distinct layers, which he calls Cucuteni A and B. The same is true for Tripolye, near Kiev, on the west side of the Dnieper, where Chvojka recognized also two layers, which are known as Tripolye A and B. A further site at Horodnica in Galicia has much in common with the earlier phases of these two sites, and is considered by most authorities to be contemporary with them.

We shall first describe the civilization of Cucuteni A, which lies just east of the Carpathians at no great distance from Erösd ; it resembles the civilization found at the latter by Laszlo so closely that all authorities are agreed that they are connected, while many believe that they are contemporary. Like Erösd this settlement lay within a fortification, consisting of a rampart of rough stone with a ditch outside it, which appears to have surrounded the village ; the ditch was deep and narrow, but during the second phase this was filled up, and another ditch, broader and shallower, was dug at some distance outside. The form of the houses could not be made out.

The pottery was for the most part painted in brownish red, outlined with black paint, on a white ground ; the chief design was a horizontal double spiral. Deep cups have been found with rounded bottoms, also bottles with lugs instead of handles and sometimes with hollow ring-feet, wide open bowls and pedestalled bowls or fruit-stands. A few sherds and one complete pot of typical spiral-meander pottery were found, showing that Cucuteni A was, in part at least, contemporary with the First Danubian civilization and not altogether out of touch with the people responsible for it. Besides these wares there have been found others in which the surface is deeply grooved and the grooves filled in with white paint ; these, too, are generally decorated with double spiral designs.

Implements of flint only were found in the bottom layer at Cucuteni and no metal was discovered ; a number of clay figurines came to light, very similar in type to those of Erösd, but of more finished execution. These, apparently, repre-

Fig. 100.   Pottery from Cucuteni A.

sented the Mother Goddess. No graves were met with, so we have no means of ascertaining the physical type of the people.

Farther to the north-west, at the extreme eastern end of Galicia, lies the settlement of Horodnica, which seems to have been, in part at least, contemporary with the lower layer at Cucuteni, for the majority of the pots have the same shape and are decorated with the same double spiral designs.   The figurines from both sites are identical. Some of the wares, however, which appear commonly at Horodnica, resemble very closely those found at a third site, or group of sites, which we must now describe.

A number of village sites near Kiev, all on the west of the Dnieper, have been explored by Chvojka, and the civilization found there has been named after the chief site, Tripolye or

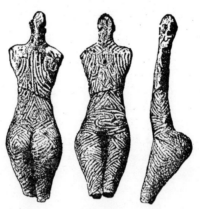

Fig. 101.   Clay figures from Cucuteni A.

Tripolje. Here, as at Cucuteni, Chvojka recognized two periods, which are known as Tripolye A and B ; most authorities are agreed that the earlier layers at both sites are contemporary.

Most of the pottery from Tripolye A is of that grooved type that was met with, though rarely, at Cucuteni A, and that appears also at Horodnica. Painted pottery was found on the sites, but it was scarce, and it has been thought that it had been imported from elsewhere and not made on the spot. The commonest shapes are tubular stands, resembling dice-boxes, and pairs of such stands, linked together by cross-pieces and with handles at the top; these are known as binocular vases. There are also large pear-shaped urns.

The huts of these people were arranged in wide circles near streams. Metal was known there, for several copper implements were found, including flat axes and a kind of small pick-

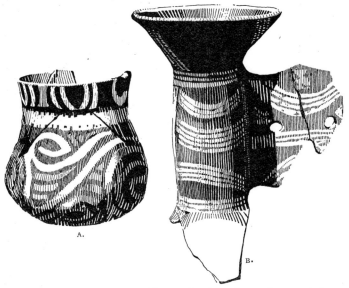

FIG. 102. Vases from Horodnica. B has been drawn, by permission, from a photograph kindly lent by Prof. Dr. Josez-ul-Kostrzewski.

axe. Perforated hammer-axes and mace-heads, as well as celts of stone, are said to have been found, and simpler tools of flint, bone, and horn. Clay figures were not common, but both erect and seated specimens were found. It is believed that the inhabitants of these settlements cultivated grain, and it is hard to believe that they could have lived in such villages were this not the case. They certainly kept domesticated animals, for bones of swine, sheep, cattle, and horses were found in plenty among their refuse. It would be unwise, however, to conclude that all these animals had been domesticated ; some, especially the horse, may have been hunted and killed for food.

There are a few other sites at which have been found pottery, very similar to the painted wares that we have been describing. These are Czernavoda in the Dobrudja, Craiova, farther west in Wallachia, and two sites in Eastern Bulgaria, Tell Ratcheff on the Tondja near Jamboli, and Tell Metchkiu near Philippopolis

FIG. 103.   Pottery from Tripolye A.

in the Maritza valley. Wares of a like nature have been reported from Eastern Macedonia, while, as we have seen, the introduction into Thessaly of pottery of this type marks the beginning of the Second Thessalian period. It has also been stated that allied wares have been met with at Hissarlik I and at the cemetery of Yortan on the Caicus ; that these wares are really connected, has, however, been disputed.

We must now consider whence came these people and their civilization. Schliz has suggested that the painted ware of Erösd was but an elaboration of certain rudely painted wares found in the Danubian region, and that from Erösd the art of painting pottery spread to Cucuteni and so to other parts of the Black Earth Lands. Childe has, however, pointed out that the roughly painted pots of the Danube, known as encrusted ware, belong to the Second Danubian civilization, which is contemporary with the second period in Thessaly, while the painted

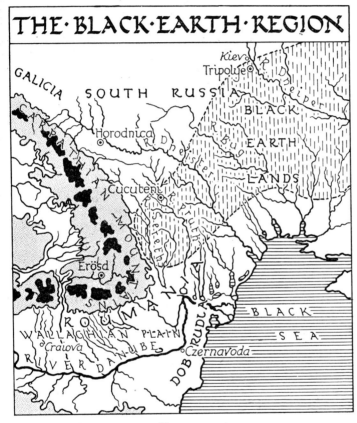

THE·BLACK·EARTH·REGION

Kiev
Tripolje
GALICIA
SOUTH RUSSIA
BLACK
Horodnica
EARTH
Cucuteni
LANDS
Erösd
ROUMANIA
WALLACHIAN PLAIN
Craiova
RIVER DANUBE
Czernavoda
DOBRUDJA
BLACK
SEA

FIG. 104.

pottery that we are discussing entered the latter area, apparently from the north, at the beginning of that period. If we accept this view, which seems to us incontestable, we must exclude from our consideration the west and the south; and since no painted wares have been found north of the Black Earth Lands we are left with the east as our only solution.

As we have seen, painted pottery was known early in Mesopotamia, at Susa, and elsewhere, and we have suspected that it reached these from some point in North Syria or south-eastern Asia Minor. It was also made at an early date at Anau in Turkestan. Recently fresh evidence of the existence of painted pottery, certainly of fairly early date, has reached us from Persia, Baluchistan, Sind, the Punjab, and from various sites in China. Some archaeologists believe that all these wares are closely connected, but their shapes and decoration are very different. At the same time it is likely that the idea of decorating pots with a coloured slip was disseminated from a common centre. It is to some subsidiary centre, in touch with the original home of this technique, that we must look for the beginnings of the wares of Erösd and Cucuteni.

No centre that will meet our needs has yet been found, but Casson has noticed, from a train window it is true, a number of flat-topped mounds on the south-eastern foot-hills of the Caucasus; these reminded him of the mounds in Turkestan like those at Anau. Childe would bring our Black Earth people thence across the Russian steppe.

While we would agree with him that the southern slopes of the Caucasus, or perhaps the northern slopes of the Armenian mountains, are an extremely likely centre for this dispersal, we do not feel convinced about the route he suggests. The western end of the Caucasus drops abruptly to the Black Sea, and a coastal route, while not impossible, would not have been inviting. Had our people passed that way it is strange that they have not left their mark in the Kuban valley, which is and must then have been very fertile. Beyond the Kuban lies a long stretch of dry steppe land, none too well watered, which would have been uninviting to grain growers. Nor was it uninhabited. Nomadic pastoral tribes, who buried their dead covered with red ochre, and whom we have called Northern Steppe-folk, roamed these steppes, and, though they may not have been hostile, it would have required some courage for strangers to trek for long distances through their steppes.

There is an alternative route, not easy but quite practicable, along the southern shore of the Black Sea. Down the mountain sides run many small rivers and streams by which the migrants could have settled. When they reached the Bosphorus they would have passed not far from Hissarlik, and, though they certainly did not settle there, some of their pots may have found their way to this village. Crossing the Bosphorus and continuing their way along the Black Sea shore they would have reached the Dobrudja, whence some could have passed northwards to Cucuteni and thence to Horodnica and Tripolye, while others could have passed westwards through Wallachia and up the Alt to Erösd, where they grew rich from the gold and copper which was to be found in that neighbourhood.

The pottery from Bulgaria is certainly somewhat later than that of Cucuteni A, and that from eastern Macedonia probably still later ; in these it seems quite correct to see evidence of the passage southwards of this culture on its way to Thessaly. It is not clear, however, that the same is true of the remains from the Dobrudja and Wallachia, which may well be evidence of the advent of painted pottery into the Black Earth Lands. Against this suggestion is the fact that no traveller has brought back from northern Anatolia any painted potsherds of this type.

As, however, no direct evidence of the line of advance is yet forthcoming, we must be content to put the two suggested routes before our readers, leaving them to take their choice ; we have already stated that at the present moment we feel inclined to prefer the latter alternative.

BOOKS

BURROWS, RONALD M.   *The Discoveries in Crete* (London, 1907).
CHILDE, V. GORDON.   *The Dawn of European Civilization* (London, 1925).
MINNS, ELLIS.   *Scythians and Greeks* (Cambridge, 1913).

II

Chronological Summary

IN this part we have been dealing with a period of a thousand years, roughly from 3500 to 2500 B.C. In the Near East it was a remarkable millennium. In Egypt it witnessed the unification of the kingdom, and the development of writing, which reached its standard form during the second half of the period. It saw, too, the introduction of building in dressed stone, and the rise of a highly organized priesthood. In Mesopotamia the advance was not so marked. Many attempts at the unification of this area under a single monarch were only partially successful and for a limited time, until the Empire of Agade was founded about 2752 B.C. The priesthood became rather a religious magistracy under the control of the king ; the development of a priestly caste came later, it seems. Here writing was well developed before the period began, as was the art of dressing stone slabs, though these were used sparingly in building owing to the scarcity of the material. Building in brick, however, had reached a high pitch of excellence at an earlier date. Both regions, however, though in different ways, made great advances in the art of sculpture and in many other aspects of civilization. At the beginning of the period Mesopotamia seems to have been

leading, but during the fourth and fifth dynasties Egypt out-
stripped her rival and reached a level of civilization that was
not surpassed until a very much later time.

Before our period opens the Sumerian cities of Mesopotamia
had been dominated by alien Elamites from Awan, but about
3500 B.C. these were expelled by the men of Kish, who established the second dynasty of that city ; this lasted for about
180 years. It was about this time, or perhaps a little earlier,
that new people arrived in Upper Egypt, possibly from the Red
Sea. If, as has been suggested, they came from the shores of the
Persian Gulf, and were allied to the Elamites, their departure
from their original home may well have coincided with that
Elamite expansion which brought to an end the first dynasty
of Ur about 3575 B.C.

The new-comers, who worshipped a Falcon deity, settled
down by the Nile in Upper Egypt among the makers of stone
bowls, and seem to have established themselves there as a ruling
caste. In the Delta the worshippers of Osiris were hemmed in
on the east by the goat-herd worshippers of Anzety and on the
west by the olive-growing Tehenu from Libya. They seem,
however, to have for a time maintained their independence,
ruling the Central Delta from their capital at Buto. Later
they were driven south to the Middle Nile, above Cairo, and
their monarch ruled at the Het-Insi, later Aphroditopolis just
south of Cairo, and adopted the white crown as part of his
regalia. Before 3400 B.C. the Tehenu, whose capital had been
at Sais, and whose kings wore the red crown, made themselves
masters of the whole of the Delta. About the same time,
however, ' The Scorpion ', the king of the Falcon worshippers,
led an army down the Nile and made himself master of Middle
Egypt, assuming the white crown. His successor Narmer, the
Menes of tradition, defeated the Tehenu, assumed the red crown

which he joined to the white, and became the first king of a united Egypt. He was the first king of the first dynasty, which ruled until about 3200 B.C.

Many of the Tehenu, resenting the usurpation of power by Narmer-Menes, left the Delta, and, if Evans's latest suggestion is correct, some of them sailed to Crete and settled there on the Mesara Plain, introducing to that island many of the elements of civilization, which they had developed in their North African home. Their arrival, about or soon after 3400 B.C., inaugurated the First Early Minoan period.

About this time a broad-headed people occupying the south-west corner of Asia Minor, known to the Greeks as Caria, began exploring the islands off their coast. They discovered obsidian in Melos, emery in Naxos, and marble in Paros; these commodities they exchanged for other products in Crete and Egypt. It is doubtful if at first they made permanent settlements in these islands, and our chief evidence for their presence is derived from isolated tombs, which might be those of visitors who died there while exploiting the wealth of these islands.

About 3320 B.C. the Elamite kings of Hamasi made another attempt to bring the Sumerian cities under their sway. This was only partially successful and their rule lasted only until about 3295 B.C. At this date a king of Erech led a successful revolt, and, moving the seat of his kingdom to Ur, established the second dynasty of that city. About this time movements were taking place in Turkestan. People from the east, bringing with them the camel and other fresh elements of culture, arrived at Anau. It is about this time, too, that we feel inclined to attribute the westward spread of the Anau culture round the south of the Caspian Sea to the region lying between the Caucasus and the Armenian mountains.

About 3200 B.C. the first dynasty came to an end in Egypt,

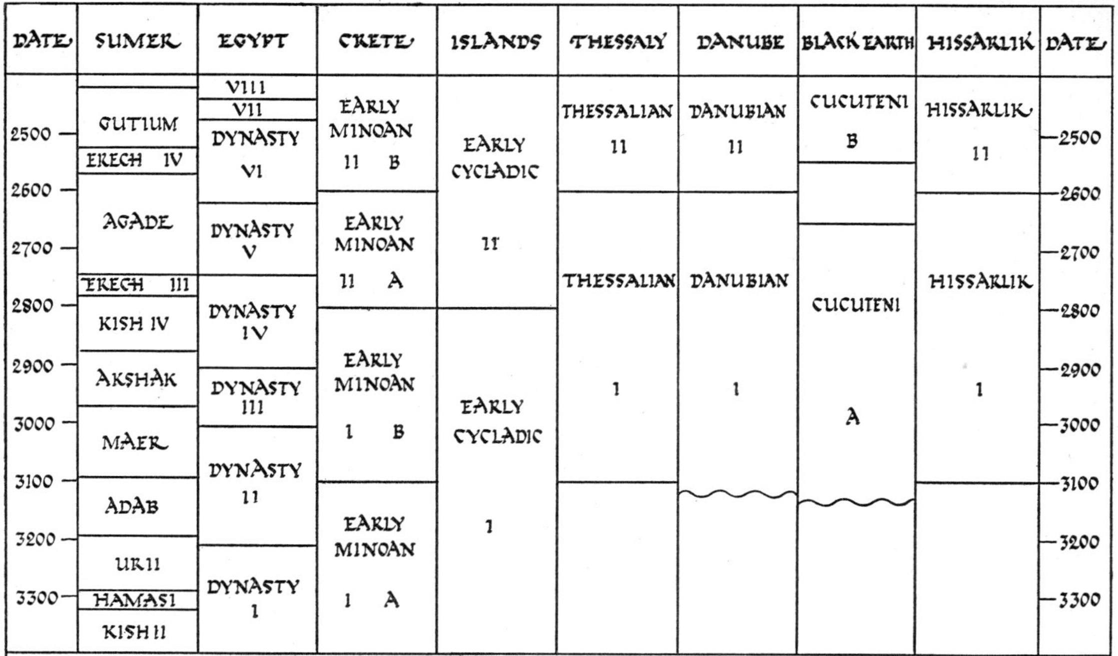

Fig. 105 General Chronological Chart

DATE	SUMER	EGYPT	CRETE	ISLANDS	THESSALY	DANUBE	BLACK EARTH	HISSARLIK	DATE
2500	GUTIUM	VIII / VII / DYNASTY VI	EARLY MINOAN II B	EARLY CYCLADIC II	THESSALIAN II	DANUBIAN II	CUCUTENI B	HISSARLIK II	2500
2600	ERECH IV								2600
2700	AGADE	DYNASTY V	EARLY MINOAN II A						2700
2800	ERECH III / KISH IV	DYNASTY IV			THESSALIAN I	DANUBIAN I	CUCUTENI A	HISSARLIK I	2800
2900	AKSHAK	DYNASTY III	EARLY MINOAN I B	EARLY CYCLADIC I					2900
3000	MAER								3000
3100	ADAB	DYNASTY II							3100
3200	UKII		EARLY MINOAN I A						3200
3300	HAMASI / KISH II	DYNASTY I							3300

Fig. 105 General Chronological Chart

Nota. The chart reads, in order of time, from the bottom upwards.

and in the second dynasty we are inclined to see the rise to power of those worshippers of Osiris, who had introduced the cultivation of wheat into the Delta. About 3187 B.C. the second dynasty of Ur gave way to one which ruled at Adab for ninety years. During this century there seem to have been various movements across Asia Minor. We have conjectured that some grain-growers, starting from the coastal lands of Pisidia, began to spread to the north-west, eventually reaching the Aegean Sea near Ephesus. About the same time others, starting perhaps from Cilicia and passing through the Cilician gorge, spread along the south of the interior plain of Asia Minor, ultimately reaching the Aegean Sea at or near the mouth of the Caicus. Lastly, we have suspected that a third group of grain-growers, who made painted pottery, left the region between the Caucasus and the Armenian mountains, passing eastward along either the southern or the northern shore of the Black Sea.

About 3097 B.C. the dynasty of Adab fell and nearly all the Sumerian city states passed into the hands of a new power, which had arisen in the steppe-lands to the north-west. These people came down the Euphrates from a city or region known as Maer, and the dynasty of Maer ruled until about 2961 B.C. During the early part of this time their rule seems to have extended over the whole Sumerian region, but before 3000 B.C. many of the cities, under the energetic leadership of Lagash, revolted and established their independence. In Crete copper, long known but scarce, came into general use, while about this time the three groups of grain-growers, whom we have suspected of spreading westward, arrived in Europe. The first group seems to have crossed the Aegean Sea by a chain of islands to the southern shore of Thessaly, and to have settled in the Thessalian plain. The second went by sea or land to the lower reaches of the Danube and, passing the Iron Gate, settled in the south-

MIGRATIONS OF THE GRAIN GROWERS

Fig. 106.

east of the Hungarian plain, where they worked deposits of copper, cinnabar, and gold, exporting the last-named metal, which eventually reached Egypt. Before 3000 B.C. the third group, with their painted pots, had reached the Rumanian plain and had settled by the upper waters of the Alt.

As we have seen the power of the dynasty of Maer was finally broken about 2961 B.C., largely by the influence of the people of Lagash, and the kings of Akshak claimed the supremacy. It is doubtful whether their rule extended over all the Sumerian city states, but they remained the leading power until about 2875 B.C. Meanwhile about 3000 B.C. Khasekhem had established himself as first king of the third dynasty in Egypt and had assumed the name of Khasekhemui. His tomb is the first building yet discovered that was built of dressed stone, and in it were discovered the fragments of gold, to which we have so often referred. His successor Zoser built the first elaborate stone temple with stone pillars and erected the first pyramids ; these were the work of his vizier, Imhotep. This wonderful man, who has passed down to posterity as the Father of Science, seems to have been responsible for the great and rapid advance that was then made in architecture and other civilized arts.

There was little change, as far as we can judge, in the civilization in Crete or Thessaly, but the people from Caria had by now made permanent settlements in the Cyclades. The mainland of Greece, south of Thessaly, seems to have been uninhabited. The folk of the painted pots had settled at Cucuteni, where they had defended themselves with a ditch and bank, while at Erösd in the Alt Valley they were probably mining copper at the source of that river and getting gold from their Danubian neighbours at Tordos. Humble settlements of fisherfolk were made near the coast of Asia Minor, especially at Hissarlik and Yortan.

The hegemony of Akshak came to an end about 2875 B.C., and Kish again rose to power ; the fourth dynasty of this city brought all the Sumerian cities under its sway. About 2900 B.C. Snefru founded the fourth dynasty in Egypt, and his successors, Khufu or Cheops and his immediate descendants, built the great pyramids of Giza. Then followed the most flourishing period of Egyptian civilization, known as that of the Old Kingdom.

The Danubian peasants increased in numbers and began spreading up the Danube and its tributaries, settling on hard patches of loess by the river-side. As they left the region of copper mines they began to depend more and more on flint tools, till at length they degenerated to the stage commonly known in the west as Neolithic. The painted pottery people of the Rumanian plain spread along the foot-hills on the outside of the Carpathians, and by the close of the century had reached the borders of Galicia. At Erösd a new influence is apparent at this time in the presence of the Megaron or porched house ; whence this came is uncertain.

Towards the close of its rule the power of the fourth dynasty of Kish was weakened by renewed activity at Lagash, a city that was always jealous of its independence. About 2777 B.C. its rule came to an end and its place was taken by Erech. The third dynasty of that city ruled most of Mesopotamia until about 2752 B.C. It was then that there arose in Kish a man who made a great mark in the ancient world. This was Sargon, who soon shifted the seat of his government to his new city of Agade. This wonderful man not only brought under his rule all the Sumerian cities of Mesopotamia and the Elamite states in the south-east, but before he had been on the throne many years had extended his empire from the Persian Gulf to the Mediterranean Sea, and had established relations with Cyprus, Crete, and the south coast of Asia Minor.

M

About 2750 B.C. the fourth dynasty in Egypt gave way to the fifth, but the high state of civilization established by Khufu and his successors continued with but little abatement. The founder of the new dynasty was High Priest of Re, apparently at Heliopolis, and from this time on we find that conjunction of the priestly and kingly office which occurred so often later on in Egyptian history. This conjunction of the two offices seems to resemble the early arrangements in the Sumerian cities, but there is this important difference. The Sumerian patesi was a magistrate who performed sacred or priestly functions; the kings of the fifth dynasty were priests who had usurped royal powers.

The Thessalian peasants, who had long occupied the fertile plain of the Peneus basin, began spreading slowly southwards, and by the close of the century had occupied most of Central Greece. The Danubians had spread northwards into Moravia, where their settlements existed beside every stream. The inhabitants of Rumania had also spread northwards, giving up the custom of painting their pottery in favour of incised designs, and had settled in large numbers on the west side of the Dnieper, in the neighbourhood of Kiev; this area is known as that of the Tripolye culture. About the end of the century disturbing influences were felt in Turkestan, and the settlement at the North Kurgan of Anau came abruptly to an end.

Sargon reigned at Agade until his death about 2697 B.C. During his later years he was called upon to suppress many revolts, but these broke out again at his death and were constant events during the reigns of his descendants. The latter succeeded, however, in keeping the government of Mesopotamia in their hands until about 2571 B.C. The priestly kings of the fifth dynasty continued in Egypt, but they delegated much of their power to the nobles, so that their rule became weaker. In 2625 B.C. they gave way to the sixth dynasty.

FIG. 107. Statue of an Egyptian princess in the Turin Museum.

In Crete civilization developed, and at this time we enter the period known as the Second Early Minoan. Trade had improved and quantities of gold and other valuables have been found in the tombs of this period. The Thessalian peasants were spreading still farther to the south, and seem to have reached the Peloponnese around Corinth and Arcadia. In Moravia the Danubians seem to have mingled with folk who hunted over the sandy wastes of North Hungary; as a result they made pots in imitation of the leather bags used by these nomad people.

About 2600 B.C., or perhaps a little later, there were disturbing elements in south-east Europe, possibly a continuation of those which brought to an end the settlement in the North Kurgan at Anau. Cucuteni and Erösd were abandoned, the fishing village at Hissarlik was destroyed, and new elements of culture entered Thessaly and Hungary. At about the same time Mesopotamia was invaded by people from the desert, while other desert tribes, and negroes from the south, were threatening the sixth dynasty in Egypt. The whole ancient world, save the islands in the Aegean Sea, was in a turmoil; the causes of this must be left for discussion in the next part.

Quite recently Dr. Frankfort has suggested fresh dates for the early periods in Greek lands. He thinks that the First Early Minoan, Cycladic, and Helladic periods began with the Late Predynastic period in Egypt, which we have placed soon after 4000 B.C., and that the second of such periods began about 3400 B.C. We reserve our judgement for the present.

The Races of the World

CLASSIFICATIONS of human races have been multiplied with little profit, and it seems almost impossible to devise any satisfactory scheme based upon a survey of modern populations alone. One can map distributions of characters such as those of the hair, the skin, the nose, or the head, but these distributions often fail to coincide, so that 'race-type' in a general sense is a very difficult matter to define. Moreover, much of the information available suffers from all the disabilities of statistical methods, for it deals in averages of large numbers of cases, and such averages, in human affairs, rarely mean very much.

The modern types of men spread in drifts over most of the land of the world in the early days of humanity and have continued to spread in later times in more organized fashion, so that we can speak of migrations. The early drifts of mankind, could we but follow them, would probably give us many clues to the modern race types and the present distribution of the physical characteristics of mankind. It is, therefore, useful to follow up the few clues available in the present state of our knowledge, and to try to see how the changes of climate and environment, sketched in earlier parts of this study, help to interpret present-day racial features.

Let us, however, bear in mind that more or less continuous drifts of beings, who are likely to intermarry, do not easily give rise to sharply marked types. In every direction we have rather a continuous mass, shading off gradually from one type to another, while in nearly every region we have differing types living side by side, with differing characters present in different individuals.

The early home of modern types of men cannot yet be placed with certainty ; we have seen reason, however, to suppose that it was in some region where temperature conditions and variations were not far from what seems to be the optimum for many peoples of our time. That optimum, so far as our little knowledge goes, seems to be much the same for many peoples ; thus it would appear to be a feature derived from more or less common ancestors. We must not, however, picture one spot with a small group of families, but rather a broad zone with somewhat different human beings in its different parts. This zone we have placed provisionally along what is now the Sahara, Arabia, and Mesopotamia ; it was a zone of winter rains in the glacial phases of the Pleistocene period, so that it was largely grassland with rivers in what are now dry valleys.

In *Hunters and Artists* we have seen reason to think that some early types of modern man, owing to additional growth of the frontal region of the brain under circumstances and limitations there discussed, became very long-headed and high-headed. It is possible to interpret some modern groups of men as survivors of types that had not undergone this change ; these were still characterized by heads of medium proportions, neither relatively very long nor very broad. Others we may think of as survivors of persons who had undergone the lengthening of the head, without any increase in its height. Lastly, others may be considered survivors of persons who had undergone increase in both the length and height of the head. The first two groups are represented in various localities which lie on the south and south-east side of the supposed zone of early modern man, while the third group has a wider and more scattered distribution.

Most of those who fall into the first group are very short

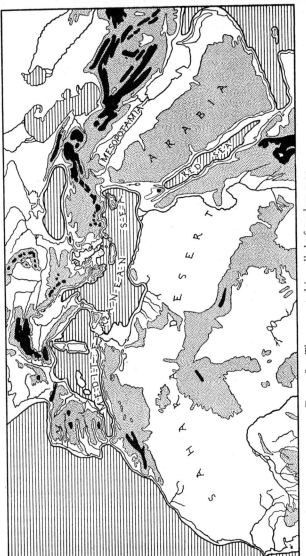

Fig. 108. The suggested 'cradle' of modern man.

with spirally curved hair, and it has recently been claimed that such hair, growing from roots near the surface of the skin, is a feature that appears about the time of birth in Africa or during infancy in Melanesia. The early pre-natal growth of hair is from deep fairly straight roots. However this may be, we may think of spirally curved hair as, in general, a specialization on the south side of the early cradle of modern types. The pre-natal hair is retained in the pigmies who dwell in the equatorial forests of Africa.

Among the peoples who retain the unlengthened head, with the ancient prominent jaws and with the spirally curved hair, we may mention the Andamanese, the Semang in the Malay Peninsula, the Aeta in the Philippines, and the Tapiro in Papua ; these are all very short and very dark with broad flat noses. It will help us to understand their spread to these regions if we reconstruct the distribution of land and water with the coast line at the present 100-fathom line or thereabouts. Under these conditions Sumatra, Java, Bali, Borneo, and Palawan would form a hooked peninsula attached to Further India. Only narrow straits would separate this peninsula from the Philippines and from the Lombok–Flores–Ombaya land, while again similar narrow straits would exist between the last named and the Timor group and between that group and a land including Papua and Australia.

In Africa the pigmies of the equatorial forest and the bushmen of the south-western desert are in many ways comparable with the peoples mentioned above, but the bushmen are slightly taller and some have longer heads. These two peoples, however, have skins that are not so dark as those of the pigmies of the East Indies. The Tasmanians, now just extinct, had moderate stature and some of them had long heads. They were very dark and had spirally curved hair and broad flat noses.

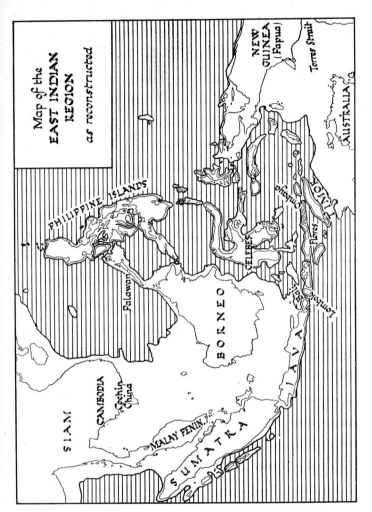

Map of the
EAST INDIAN
REGION
as reconstructed

PHILIPPINE ISLANDS

NEW
GUINEA
(Papua)

Torres Strait

AUSTRALIA

TIMOR

Ombay

Flores

CELEBES

Palawan

Lombok

Bali

SIAM

CAMBODIA

Cochin
China

MALAY PENIN.?

BORNEO

SUMATRA

JAVA

FIG. 109.

In contradistinction to most of the peoples we have mentioned, they had strong brow ridges, a feature, like the great head length frequently found among them, which indicates greater or longer continued growth than that of the pigmies. The Papuans often have very long and high heads with spirally curved hair, not quite identical, apparently, with that of the African negro population, which is, also, typically long-headed and often high-headed as well.

While spirally curved hair is a feature of the peoples who may be thought to have spread southward into Africa from the supposed early home, that characteristic is found only in some of the spreads towards the south-east. It seems probable that an element with very dark skin and spirally curved hair may have influenced some dark types in South India, but there and among the Vedda of Ceylon wavy to curly hair is the rule. These people are typically long-headed and relatively high-headed. The same combination of dark skin, wavy to curly hair, and long heads occurs also in Australia, where in the south-east the heads are often low, while in the north they are predominantly high. In all these the mouth is large and projects forwards ; the stature is usually moderate.

It is not only on the south side of the cradle of men of modern type that we find survivals of early stages of their evolution. On the north side, however, we do not find the spirally curved hair in modern times, though one of the Aurignacian statuettes from Willendorf in Austria seems to portray it. In remote corners of western Europe from Portugal to Norway, as well as in several other more or less inaccessible places in southern and central Europe and in North Africa, one finds men with very long and high heads. These features are associated with dark hair and eyes ; often with a dark tinge in the skin. Some show the strong brow ridges of one early type, others show the smooth forehead of another, but no one can fail to see that the persons concerned exhibit survivals of the ancient characters discussed in *Hunters and Artists*. Many of

Fig. 110. The Plynlymon type.

Photograph by Mr. L. H. Dudley Buxton, reproduced by his kind permission.

these nests of old-fashioned types are probably related to a drift northwards through western Europe during the retreat of the ice-sheets, when the land stood higher than now, and the British Isles were a peninsula. Another drift, however, must be noticed.

The home-zone of early modern man must have been closed
on the north so long as the ice-sheets remained large, but, as
they diminished, a way would open between the Hindu Kush
and the Elburz mountains into the steppe of Turkestan and
beyond. Drifts in this direction could spread westwards, north
of the Caspian and Black Seas into the loess belt that extends
westwards into Europe ; or they could spread, too, north-eastwards to the north-east of Asia, avoiding at first the high east-
central Asiatic plateau. The north-eastward drift reached
America. With this in mind one can understand that there
are survivors of old types of very long-headed men in corners
of America remote from Alaska, either among living persons or
among burials of not very ancient date. Some features of these
types occur among the Eskimo, the peoples of the east Brazilian
plateau, and in other places. They also occur among the Ainu
of North Japan and on the Asiatic mainland near by. These
survivals are not to be considered as a race or races apart, but
rather as the earliest and farthest drifts of a more or less continuous spread from the early cradle and from the zones opened
up successively as man's equipment and opportunities improved.
They need not in all cases be of very ancient standing in their
present homes.

Far more numerous than these survivals of early types are
the representatives of those whom we have supposed to show
more general growth, growth both in breadth and in length of
head, but especially in the latter. These are the moderately
long-headed people, whose measurements on the living head
show the breadth to be from 74 to 79 per cent. of the length.
In these the brow ridges are rarely as strong as they are in many
of the people interpreted above as survivors of ancient types,
but amongst them a few such survivors may be found in most
places. Typical of these are the peoples living around the

western Mediterranean basin, the wavy-haired peoples of North Africa, the Semitic peoples of the Arabian desert and its borders, some elements of the population of the Persian plateau, and the general population of the Deccan, known as Dravidian, with its extensions over the East Indian Archipelago and beyond. These various regional groups differ from one another in various ways, being relatively dark in the Deccan, a rich brown in Arabia and North Africa, and of rather an olive tinge around the western Mediterranean and in the Aegean islands. Their home areas are apparently penetrated in most places by broad-headed types, which will be discussed later in this chapter.

In addition to this main belt of moderately long-headed people we find corresponding elements among the native peoples of America and among the peoples of the provinces of China, as well as in Japan and North-east Asia. There is thus no doubt that persons with this form of head took part in the series of north-eastward drifts from the early cradle above discussed.

A north-westward drift of this kind, probably through Persia to Turkestan and thence to Europe, but just possibly also through Asia Minor and Thrace, needs further consideration. The kurgans of South Russia have yielded numerous skeletons, nearly all of long-headed men, and including a fair proportion, about ten to twelve per cent., of survivals of the old very long and high-headed characters ; these kurgans are of many periods but some may be very old. The kurgans of Turkestan are still almost unknown, but one at Anau has yielded some skeletons of moderately long-headed people and it may be provisionally dated not far from 3000 B.C. A north-westward spread of very long-headed people, and of moderately long-headed people too, may thus be supposed to have occurred, starting from the eastern part of what has been called the early cradle. This spread apparently reached the Baltic lands and formed the

basis of the ' Nordic race ' so often discussed at the present
time. North-western conditions seem to have been such as to
discourage the development of pigment in the skin, hair, and
eyes ; and the colouring here is generally fair, with the eyes

FIG. 111.   An American Indian from the plains.

*Photograph by Mr. L. H. Dudley Buxton reproduced by kind
permission of the Editor from ' Discovery ', 1925.*

blue or grey.   It should, however, be noticed that some very
long-headed people with darker hair and eyes occur in Norway,
and that the fully blond type is not so general in that country
as is sometimes supposed.   It occurs most characteristically
near Trondhjem Fjord, a district with more extensive lowland
than is found elsewhere in West Norway, and a district readily

accessible from Sweden through the Stor valley. This way from Sweden may have played a considerable part in the spread of men of this kind to Norway.

The question of the types of people in the British Isles has received separate treatment from one of us, and here we may content ourselves with the suggestion that in the British Isles there are what seem to be survivors of types belonging to early drifts of men up the west coast of Europe, as stated earlier in this chapter, and to early drifts along the north-westward spread just mentioned. A large element in the population is moderately long-headed, with rather fair skin but brown hair, along with eyes typically brown or grey, though in some cases blue. That absolutely fair types have spread into Britain across the North Sea in prehistoric as well as historic times seems hardly to admit of question.

In the introductory paragraphs of this chapter reference was made to the possibility that some early types of modern men did not show the great relative lengthening of the head that was said to be characteristic of others. It is useful, as a provisional hypothesis, to think that such men, with heads of an index indicating a medium breadth, about seventy-nine to eighty-two on the living head, occurred not only, as stated in those introductory paragraphs, on the south side of the early home-zone but also on the north. If we further suppose that in this cool climate they participated, along with the long-headed folk, in the improvement of general growth, we can form some idea of the early stages in the spread of what are called the broad-headed races of man.

Broad-headedness is now most characteristic of the belt of highlands in the northern hemisphere from the Pyrenees to North-east Siberia, and the belt is continued all along the highlands of West America from Alaska to Patagonia. The belt of broad-headedness includes regions where very broad heads, with an index of eighty-five and upwards, are frequent, and it seems probable that these types of head with remarkable relative breadth have developed from ancestral types with the more moderate indices noted just previously. How and why they have thus developed are biological questions to which as yet only very tentative answers have been given, but two of these regions of extreme relative breadth of head must be mentioned. One of these is Armenia and Asia Minor, with extensions into the Balkan Peninsula on the Illyrian side. In this region the head is short and high, and the profile is remarkably developed with a nose outstanding, to quote the Song of Songs ' as the tower of Lebanon that looketh toward Damascus '.

Professor Thomson and others think large nasal chambers often accompany a broad high head. On the highland areas north and north-east of Tibet, including the Tarim basin and the Gobi Desert, the head is, on the other hand, relatively low and rounded with, in many individuals, flattened features and the additional or ' Mongolian ' fold of the eyelid. In this region and among these types the cheek-bone is flattened and deepened and this gives extra directness to, as well as additional space for, the attachment of the chewing or masseter muscles. With this flattening seems to have gone a flattening of the nasal bones, so that space for large nasal chambers has to be found well in towards the brain instead of by forward projection. This mode of growth seems to have helped to push out the cheek-bones and to have promoted growth in head-breadth. In the Carpathians, the Alps, and the Central Plateau of France the broad-heads have mostly a rounded form with moderately prominent noses ; here and there in remote spots the relative breadth is much exaggerated, apparently, in some cases, as a result of inbreeding.

The skin among the broad-heads of the mountain zone is generally thought to be rather dry and opaque, but this character is most highly developed among the people with flattened features and very broad heads on the highlands north and north-east of Tibet.   Here the skin is compact, rich in dry outer

Fig. 112.   An Asiatic Alpine from Turkestan.

layers, and almost hairless save on the head, while its bloodvessels are deep set, so that the pink colour rarely shows and the tint is typically yellow-brown.   These characters of the skin bear a fairly clear relation to the climatic conditions with their long bitter dry anticyclones of winter.

We may for the present, then, think of broad-headed men evolving not from the early long-heads but rather from ancestors who did not undergo that lengthening process to any great extent, ancestors who lived on the north and north-east flank of what we have called the early cradle, and spread thence especially in the highland belt of the northern hemisphere. It is quite possible that the highland north and north-east of Tibet was occupied only relatively late by modern types of man, as it must have been almost uninhabitable while the ice-sheets were still large.

We must also think of spreads of broad-headed man following and at times pressing upon the long-headed populations already discussed, and it seems likely that intermarriages between long heads and broad-heads result in a preponderance of broad-headed offspring, so that broad-headedness spreads, as it were, even without displacement of population. It is characteristic of large areas in France, Germany, and North Italy in Europe, and throughout these one has the impression that it has spread from the highland zone.

In one way or another the steppe of western Asia, Russian Turkestan, has become markedly broad-headed. The view is widely held, though not as yet fully established, that here there has been a displacement of people, and that this was an immense feature in the days of the dawn of history. Indo-Aryans poured into India, Kassites and others into Mesopotamia, bringing with them the horse as a companion in war and the chase. The high-caste types of North-west India are mostly very long-headed, but otherwise they do not show many characters of ancient survivals ; in particular they have long, thin, straight noses. It is quite possible that some of the kurgan skeletons of South Russia are akin to these people, and that they thus form a part of the basis of what has become in North Europe the Nordic Race. This brief sketch cannot do more than indicate the general view that the early movements of mankind will

Fig. 113. A Mongol.

probably be found to give increasingly useful clues to the evolution and distribution of the types of modern man. A few words in conclusion on the types of each of the continents may serve to clear up points in this chapter that have perhaps been difficult to follow.

Africa is the home of dark supple skin with, in some cases, abundance of blood-vessels just below the surface. This type of skin is apparently unfavourable to general hair growth, but that growth is found on the head with what seems to be marked specialization ; the roots are curved and lie near the surface and the hair grows in a close spiral. The head is usually long and there are peoples who have it very long indeed ; there are also others, such as the pigmies, which seem to show a condition prior to that growth in length. There are also more ordinary broad-heads of doubtful origin. The drying of the Sahara may have been a great factor in pressing southward and in partially isolating those who went south, at any rate till men became fairly strongly organized and equipped. Since that stage was reached, men from the north have pressed southward, and great areas are inhabited by people who combine traits that are of great antiquity in intertropical Africa with others that have come in from the north. Many Zulus are specially good illustrations of these combinations. Most of the peoples of intertropical and South Africa have no development of brow ridges, but these are found in a few cases, as among the Koranas of South Africa, who show many features of early modern man.

Australian natives illustrate a survival of an early type, and it is an open question whether they show traces of inheritance from an earlier population of Tasmanian type.

India shows traces of black skin and spirally curved hair in a few individuals, but the majority grade from survivals of early very long-headed, wavy-haired, broad-nosed dark types in parts of the south, through moderately long-headed people on the Deccan, to the very long-headed but thin-nosed tall and lightly tinted people of the north and north-west. There are also broad-headed peoples in Baluchistan and western India, who have apparently come in from farther west.

Fig. 114. A Zulu girl.

The Mongolian plateau and its borders are a home of broad-headedness, and many of the inhabitants show the flattened facial features and the folded eyelid, but there are here also peoples with strong noses. The fold of the eyelid is a very variable feature. Along the northward Siberian valleys towards the Arctic tundra of North-west Asia and North Europe occur variations of the broad-headed flat-featured type, but towards the north and north-east less broad-headed types survive. In Yezo (= Hokkaido, the north island of Japan), Sakhalin, and on the adjacent mainland are also rather long-headed men, who here show, especially among the Ainu, an unparalleled development of body hair in the males. These areas of longer heads surround the great region of the broad-heads, and the longer-headed people are in all probability survivals of the earlier drifts. In the same way one finds groups of longer-headed men more or less on the outskirts of China ; in the north these show also a reduction of the brown pigment, so that the skin appears yellow, since the blood-vessels lie deep and are hidden, while the dry layers are strongly developed. This yellowness, masked by brown, is apparently characteristic of the people of the Mongolian plateau, but it diminishes through Turkestan towards Europe.

In the island festoons of East Asia we note that the population of Japan includes Ainu in Yezo and immigrant conquerors from Korea and North China, with some underlying element from the islands farther south. The Malay Peninsula and the East Indian Archipelago were a large land mass broken by a few narrow straits in early human times, and in this region one finds not only traces of very dark pigmies with spirally curved hair but also of early types of long-heads, obviously akin to those of South India as well as to the peoples of South China. Between South-east China and the East Indies there has probably been much movement to and fro.

East of the Archipelago, in Papua and Melanesia, are probably traces of very dark pigmies, and also of taller men with the hair spirally curved and the head often very long and narrow. Polynesian peoples are for the most part akin to those of India and the East Indies, and there are indications of old very long and high-headed types, as for example in the interior of the islands of Fiji. The later waves in the peopling of Melanesia seem to have been more or less organized migrations.

For America we note first the outstanding importance of the Alaskan entry and of the route of migration along and near the great Cordilleran systems. Long high heads are known from burials and from modern peoples in various places which are mostly on the outskirts, and from these one grades to broad heads in the Cordilleran region. A few people in Mexico, for example, have something of the flattening of facial features characteristic of the Mongolian plateau ; these may be late arrivals. The greater part of the population is, however, marked by strong features. The skin often has the reddish tinge in the brown which is common in Arctic Asia, but this cannot be said to be universal.

A knowledge of stone-grinding, of the potter's art, and of some form of weaving is very widespread as an ancient feature in America, and this indicates that in all probability the drift to America occurred when these arts were being developed in the Old World. The further developments of American civilizations are a matter of dispute between those who think them indigenous, those who believe them to have been introduced by the later waves of immigrants through Alaska, and those who believe them to have been introduced by maritime immigrants from South-east Asia across Polynesia. This is not the place to enlarge upon this controversy, but we may indicate that on the whole the second view seems the most probable, especially when we reflect that stone-grinding and pottery-making are now very widely thought to have begun as part of an Old-World civilization that also included weaving and the beginnings of metal working. It was based upon early stages of the arts of cultivating wheat and barley and of domesticating animals, but these were unknown in Columbus's day in America. It should be remembered, however, that peoples traversing North-east Asia and Alaska could probably neither maintain herds of sheep, cattle or horses, nor cultivate wheat or barley. In America they found no domesticable animals save the llama and its allies in the southern part of the Cordillera, and some fowls, but they did find maize and other plants which lent themselves to cultivation, as well as herds of bison and other beasts for hunting. Hunting and cultivation, but only a little herding of special animals, are thus a feature of native American life.

For Europe we have a late palaeolithic population of various types of long-heads connected, so far as our evidence allows us to speak, with the loess and the Mediterranean basin. The probability is that broad-headed peoples spreading from Anatolia occupied the central mountain zone of Europe as it became increasingly free of ice.

The various long-headed types in the Mediterranean basin, especially in the west, show an olive tinge in the skin with dark hair and eyes, and often comparative slightness of build ; they are known as the Mediterranean race. Those who live nearer the Sahara on the south side of the Mediterranean have more red brown in the skin, and because of this and of other features they are often distinguished as the Hamitic race. To the east of these, in and around Arabia, a kindred long-headed stock, rather taller, with more marked facial features, is miscalled the Semitic race.

The various types, fundamentally long-heads but also broad-heads, north of the great mountain zone of Europe, especially around the Baltic, show striking diminution of pigmentation, and the less broad-headed among them are known as the Nordic race. Diminution of pigmentation, carried less far, is a feature of all European peoples.

The broad-heads of the central plateau of France, the Alps, the Bohemian massif, and parts of the Carpathians have a short, thickset build and for the most part a rounded head. Those of the regions near the South-east Carpathians and the Illyrian ranges, like those of Anatolia, have the head short and high,

FIG. 115. The Mediterranean type.   Portrait of himself by Rafael.
Uffizi Gallery.   Rischgitz Collection.

frequently with the back remarkably planed, and among them the facial features are often very strongly marked.

Such indications as exist point to the replacement of a long-headed by a broad-headed population in Turkestan, and it seems likely that the Kassite invaders of Babylonia, the Indo-Aryan invaders of northern India, the Lolos and No Su of Szechuan in West China are remnants of a spread of long-headed warriors from the region of Turkestan ; it is even possible that the Hyksos, or Shepherd Kings, who conquered Egypt in the second millennium, were part of the same spread. Everywhere they seem to have brought the horse as a companion in war.

This chapter cannot do more than touch upon a large and interesting problem, which will be found set out in somewhat greater detail in the *Advancement of Science* volume for 1926 and in the corresponding *Report of the British Association for the Advancement of Science,* 1926. It is inserted here to suggest that the study of the phases of civilization and the investigation of man's relations to climate, present and past, are likely to prove in the end the best clues to the present distribution of the physical types of mankind. Though several names in common use have been introduced here and there, it has been our endeavour to avoid any attempt at a classification of mankind. We have preferred to picture drifts and, in a few cases, more or less organized migrations, and to think of populations as forming a continuous series as regards physical characters. Sharp distinctions are artificial in our opinion, but the interplay of heredity and environment, especially through influences during growth, contributes in course of time to the evolution of regional types. These may show characters accumulated from diverse ancestors as well as modifications directly or indirectly due to environmental influences.

BOOKS

DENIKER, J.   *The Races of Man* (London, 1900).
FLEURE, H. J.   *The Races of England and Wales* (London, 1923).
FLEURE, H. J.   *The Peoples of Europe* (London, 1922).
HADDON, A. C.   *The Races of Man* (Cambridge, 1924).
RIPLEY, W. Z.   *The Races of Europe* (London, 1900).

INDEX

A-AN-NI-PAD-DA, 22, 24.
Abusir, 65, 76, 77, 89.
Abydos, 61, 63, 65, 68–70, 72.
Achaeans, 130.
Adab, 24, 27, 39, 42, 44, 173, 174.
Adriatic Sea, 138, 175.
Aegean islands, 38, 173, 189.
Aegean Sea, 12, 97, 98, 111–17, 124, 133, 149–52, 174, 175, 180.
Aeta, 184.
Africa, 99, 109, 172, 184, 186, 189, 196.
Agade, 25, 27, 39, 54–60, 170, 173, 177, 178.
Aha Men, 69, 81.
Ainu, 198.
Akkad, 27, 38, 39, 54, 56, 58.
Akki, 55.
Akshak, 24, 27, 39, 43, 46–50, 52, 173, 176, 177.
Akurgal, 46.
Alaska, 188, 191, 199, 200.
Áldózo, 145.
Al Murra, 64.
Alps, 25, 138, 139, 192, 200.
Alt, 15, 153–5, 157–60, 169, 176.
Aluta, 154.
Amal-Ishdagal, 57.
Amenhotep I, 30.
America, 188, 189, 191, 199, 200.
American Indian, 190.
Ammizaduga, 19, 20, 23.
amulets, 42.
Anatolia, 54, 62, 82, 83, 99, 124, 149, 150, 152, 169, 200, 201.
Anau, 133–7, 168, 172, 178, 180, 189.
Andamanese, 184.
antimony, 14.
Antiparos, 113, 122.
Anzety-folk, 62, 70, 171.
Aphroditopolis, 63, 65, 171.
Arabia, 13, 39, 63–5, 88, 182, 183, 189, 200.
Arahsamnu, 19.
Arcadia, 113, 118, 126, 180.
arch, 86.
Arghana, 12.
Argolis, 113, 118, 120, 122.
Armenia, 168, 172, 174, 192.
Armenoid type, 83, 84.
arrow-head, 7, 14.
Asclepius, 72.
Ashmolean Museum, 20, 23.
Ashur, 39, 56.
Asia, 188, 189, 194, 197–200.
Asia Minor, 13, 15, 38, 97, 99, 104, 101–13, 117, 122, 124, 128, 142, 149, 152, 168, 172–7, 189, 192.
Asine, 113, 120.
Assiût, 63, 65.
Assuan, 63, 65.
Assyria, 17, 56.
Atoti, 81.

Australia, 184–6, 196.
Austria, 138, 139, 142, 186.
Awan, 24, 27, 38, 40, 43, 171.
Azag-Bau, 52.
Azupirani, 55.

BABYLON, 18–20, 27, 39, 54, 56.
Babylonia, 17, 25, 28, 202.
Badarians, 65, 89.
Badtibira, 39.
Bagdad, 39.
Bahrein Islands, 66.
Balanbanya, 154, 155.
Bali, 184, 185.
Balkan mountains, 150.
Balkan peninsula, 192.
Baltic Sea, 189, 200.
Baluchistan, 168, 197.
barley, 134, 200.
Bavaria, 138, 139.
beads, 8, 10, 11, 42.
Behdet, 82.
Bel, 18.
Belgrade, 145, 149.
Berlin, 31.
Berosus, 18.
Beshkid mountains, 138, 140.
Bet Khallaf, 86.
Black Earth Lands, 161, 166–9, 173.
Black Sea, 13, 139, 150, 151, 167–9, 174, 175, 188.
Boeotia, 120.
Bohemia, 138–42, 144, 201.
Boner, C., 154.
Borchardt, L., 34, 77.
Borneo, 184, 185.
Bosphorus, 169.
Bow, Land of the, 65.
Boz Euyuk, 145.
Brasov or Brasso, 154, 155.
Brazil, 188.
British Isles, 187, 191.
British Museum, 20, 21, 45, 49.
bronze, 7, 10, 12–15, 80, 89, 104.
bronze age, 7, 11, 14, 98.
Buda Pest, 138, 140.
Bug, 167.
Bulgaria, 150, 166, 169.
Burrows, R. M., 170.
Buto, 62, 63, 65, 82, 171.
Buxton, L. H. Dudley, 187, 190.

CAICUS, 149, 166, 174.
Cairo, 62, 63, 65, 69, 70, 80, 88, 171.
Cambodia, 185.
camel, 134.
Caphtor, 56.
Capsian culture, 151.
Caria, 112, 113, 121, 122, 172, 175, 176.
Carmel, Mount, 80.

carnelian, 137.
Carpathians, 14, 138, 139, 155, 161, 162, 167, 177, 192, 201.
Caspian Sea, 13, 172, 188.
Casson, S., 168.
cattle, 126, 132, 133, 141, 156, 166, 200.
Caucasus mountains, 168, 172, 174.
Cedar-land, 56.
Celebes, 185.
Censorinus, 28.
Cephissus, 113, 126.
Ceylon, 186.
Chaeronea, 118.
Chalandriani, 117.
Chaldaea, 18.
Cheeseman, Major, R.E., 64.
Cheops, 73, 74, 81, 177.
Chephren, 81.
Chicago, 42, 93.
Childe, V. Gordon, 111, 133, 145, 149, 152, 153, 161, 166, 170.
China, 168, 189, 198, 202.
Chios, 113, 124.
Chipiez, C., 87.
Chronology, 16, 17, 19, 27, 36, 38.
Chvojka, 164.
Cilician gate, 56, 174.
cinnabar, 138, 153, 176.
Cochin China, 185.
Columbus, Christopher, 200.
copper, 7–15, 57, 61, 66, 73, 77, 80, 88, 99–105, 117, 132–8, 152, 153, 157, 165, 169, 174, 176.
Cordillera mountains, 199, 200.
Corinth, 113, 118, 120, 126, 180.
Craiova, 166, 167.
Crawford, O. G. S., 64.
Crete, 32, 36, 38, 56, 89, 97–123, 153, 156, 170–80.
Čsik, 154, 155.
Cucuteni, 162–9, 173, 176, 180.
Cybele, 109.
Cyclades, 38, 99, 103, 109–23, 128, 132, 175, 176.
Cycladic periods, 38, 112–21, 130, 173, 180.
cylinder seals, 64.
Cyprus, 12, 13, 56, 57, 110, 177.
Cypselus, 55.
Cyrus, 55.
Czecho-Slovakia, 140.
Czernavoda, 166, 167.

DAMASCUS, 192.
Danube basin, 14, 123–6, 138–62, 166, 167, 173–80.
Dardanelles, 129.
Dashur, 65, 73.
Dati-Enlil, 60.
Dead Sea, 65.
Deccan, 189, 197.
Dedkere Isesi, 81.
deer, 126.
Delaporte, L., 60.
Deluge, the, 22.
Den, 81.
Deniker, J., 202.

Denmark, 148.
desert, 63, 88.
Dhimini, 147.
Diarbekr, 12, 13.
Dilmun, 56, 57, 66.
Dnieper, 164, 167, 178.
Dniester, 167.
Dobrudja, 166, 167, 169.
dog, 135.
Dörpfeld, W., 130.
Dravidian peoples, 189.
Dudu, 60.

EANNATUM, 46–9.
East Indies, 184, 185, 189, 198.
Egypt, 13–17, 25–8, 32, 35–8, 61–5, 69–72, 77, 80–2, 89, 93, 96–101, 105, 110, 114, 153, 170–3, 176–80, 202.
Egyptians, 10, 25, 28, 36, 64, 66, 74, 83–7, 91, 93, 96.
Elam, 27, 39, 49, 56, 58, 60.
Elamites, 40, 43, 48, 54, 57, 58 ,171, 172 ,177
Elburz mountains, 188.
emery, 114, 117.
Enakalli, 47, 49.
Enannatum I, 46, 49, 50.
Enannatum II, 50.
Enbi-Ashtar, 40.
Enetarzi, 50.
Enezib Merpeba, 81.
Engilsa, 58.
England, 14, 202.
En-Ka—, 78.
Enlil, 42.
Enlitarzi, 50.
Ensag-kus-anna, 40.
Entemena, 50, 51.
Enugduanna, 40.
Ephesus, 113, 124, 174, 175.
Erech, 25, 27, 38, 40, 46, 52, 54, 60, 172, 173 177.
Eridu, 38.
Erösd, 153–63, 166, 168, 169, 176, 177, 180
Erzeroum, 12.
Eskimo, 188.
Euboea, 113, 116, 118.
Euphrates, 12, 13, 38–44, 50, 55, 56, 124, 174.
Europe, 17, 38, 111, 112, 133, 139, 142, 148–53, 156–61, 170, 171, 180, 186–94, 197–202.
Eusebius, 18, 25.
Evans, Sir Arthur, 32, 34, 36, 38, 98–101, 109, 111, 172.

FALCON-FOLK, 66, 68, 171.
Falcon-kings, 70.
Fayûm, 65.
Fertile Crescent, 12, 14.
Field Museum, Chicago, 42.
Fiji, 199.
Fleure, H. J., 202.
flint, 7, 14, 61, 136, 156.
Flood, the, 22, 24, 25, 27.
Forsdyke, E. J., 122.
Fotheringham, J. K., 20.
France, 14, 192, 194, 200.
Frankfort, H., 64, 66, 144, 180.

GALICIA, 145, 161–3, 167, 177.
Gebel El Arak, 64.
Geer, Baron de, 16.
Germany, 139, 194.
Gimil, 24.
Gimil-durul, 60.
Gimil-Sin, 52.
Giza, 65, 73–6, 83–5, 177.
Glotz, G., 111, 114, 133.
goats, 132, 156.
Gobi desert, 192.
gold, 8, 14, 15, 104, 117, 138, 153–7, 169, 176, 180.
Gournia, 104.
grain, 101, 114, 126, 128, 156.
Great Britain, 39.
Greece, 97, 112, 113, 118, 124, 161, 176, 178, 180.
Greeks, 25, 57, 61, 72, 113, 170, 172.
Gschnitz glaciation, 25.
Gu-edin, 46, 47, 50.
Gunidu, 45.
Guroar, 45.
Gutium, 27, 60, 173.
Gyŏr County, 145.

HADANIS, 40.
Haddon, A. C., 202.
Hagia Marina, 118.
Hagia Triada, 100.
Hall, H. R., 22, 30, 32, 34, 35, 38, 60, 96.
Halonnesos, 113, 124.
Hamasi, 24, 27, 38, 40, 43, 172, 173.
Heliopolis, 65, 70, 76, 96, 178.
Helladic periods, 38, 112–15, 120, 121, 180.
Hellas, 112, 113.
Hellespont, 113, 124, 149, 150, 152.
Heriu-Sha, 80.
Herodotus, 96.
Heskiu, 63.
Hetepeth-eres or Hetep-here, 73.
Het-Insi, 63, 171.
Hieraconpolis, 65, 88.
Hindu Kush, 188.
hippopotamus, 63.
Hissarlik, 112–15, 123, 124, 129–32, 145, 149, 157, 166, 169, 173–6, 180.
Hokkaido, 198.
Homer, 130.
Horodnica, 162–5, 167, 169.
horse, 69, 82.
Horus, 68, 82.
Horus name, 69.
Hotepsekhemui, 81.
Hugyaj, 145.
Hungary, 139, 140, 143, 145, 146, 160, 176, 180.
Hyksos, the, 26, 202.

IBARIM, 57.
Ice Age, 16.
Ieonium, 149.
Ida, Mount, 108, 109.
Ila-Shamash, 44.
Ili, 50.

Illyria, 192, 201.
Imnotep, 70, 76, 176.
Imouthes, 72.
India, 184, 186, 194, 196, 198, 202.
Indo–Aryans, 194, 202.
Insi, 63, 69.
Inti, 78.
Ireland, 14.
iron, 36, 80.
Iron Age, 7.
Iron Gate, 138, 139, 174, 175.
ishakku, 44.
Isin, 20, 22, 27.
Italy, 14, 111, 118, 175, 194.

JABRIN, 64.
Jamboli, 166.
Japan, 188, 189, 198.
Java, 184, 185.
Judaea, 65, 84.
Julius Africanus, 18, 25.

KA, 98.
Kahun papyrus, 30, 31, 34.
Kakau, 76.
Kalathiana, 107.
Kaptara, 56, 57.
Karker, 50.
Ka Sen, 81.
Kassites, 27, 194, 202.
Khabur, 39, 44.
Khafre, 76, 81, 94.
Khamazi, 38, 40.
Khaneferre, 81.
Khasekhem, 70, 90, 176.
Khasekhemui, 14, 15, 70, 72, 81, 83, 84, 90, 104, 153, 176.
Khotan, 137.
Khufu, 73–6, 81, 84, 85, 177, 178.
Kiev, 162, 164, 167, 178.
King, L. W., 49, 60.
Kish, 22–5, 27, 39–43, 46–9, 52–5, 66, 148, 149, 171, 173, 177.
Knossos, 32, 38, 98, 100, 111, 113.
Korakou, 118.
Koranas, 196.
Korea, 198.
Koronczo, 145.
Kostrewski, J., 165.
Kronstadt, 154.
Ku, 57.
Kuban, 168.
Kug-Bau, 24.
Kuga-ki or Ku-ki, 56, 57.
Kugler, F. X., 19, 20.
Kurshesh, 58.

LAGASH, 38, 41, 45–50, 53, 54, 56, 58 64 67, 174, 176, 177.
Laipum, 55.
Langdon, S., 22, 57, 60, 66.
lapsi lazuli, 137.
Larak, 39.
Larsa, 38, 46.
Laszlo, F., 154–60, 162.
lead, 13, 117, 136.

Lebanon, 56, 86, 89, 192.
Legrain, L., 20.
Lengyel, 138, 146.
Libya, 109, 171.
Libyans, 62, 66, 80.
Lidda, 46.
Ligurian caves, 111.
Lolos, 202.
Lombok-Flores-Ombaya land, 184, 185.
Louvre, The, 49.
Lower Sea, 56, 57.
lugal, 44.
Lugal-anda, 50, 52.
Lugal-dalu, 42.
Lugal-ezen, 46.
Lugal-mundu, 42.
Lugal-shagengur, 41.
Lugal-zaggisi, 53–5.
Lummurdur, 50.

MACEDONIA, 113, 124, 166, 169.
mace-heads, 64.
Mackay, E., 42.
Maer, 24, 27, 39, 44–9, 54, 173, 174, 176.
Maganna, 56, 57.
malachite, 10.
Malay Peninsula, 184, 185, 198.
Manetho, 25, 26, 61, 74.
Manishtissu, 58.
March, 138, 140.
Maritza, 149, 166.
Marmora, Sea of, 151.
Maros, 15, 138, 146, 153–5, 157.
mastaba, 83.
Mebasi, 42.
Mediterranean race, 151, 152, 200, 201.
Mediterranean Sea, 13, 14, 56, 65, 85, 110,
    111, 142, 143, 151, 177, 183, 189, 200.
Medûm, 73, 74, 89.
Melanesia, 184, 198, 199.
Melos, 97, 99, 113, 114, 126, 128, 172, 175.
Memphis, 65, 69, 70, 84, 91, 96.
Menes, 26, 34, 69, 81, 82, 89, 99, 171
Menkauhor, 81.
Menkaure, 76, 81.
Menkers, 80.
Merenre Mehtimsaf I, 80.
Merenre Mehtimsaf II, 80.
Meritiotis, 73.
Merpeba, 69, 81.
Mes-an-ni-pad-da, 22, 24.
Mesara, 99, 101, 105, 111, 113, 172, 175.
Mesilim, 40, 41, 47, 49.
Mesolithic Age, 17.
Mesopotamia, 13, 17, 22, 25–7, 38, 39, 54,
    56, 60, 64, 69, 97, 104, 168, 170, 171, 177–3,
    194.
metal, 7, 8, 12, 13, 36.
Mexico, 199.
Meyer, E., 34, 35.
Miamu, 111.
Minns, E., 170.
Minoan periods, 36–8, 98–105, 109–15, 122,
    130, 172, 173, 180.
Minos, 36, 38, 98, 111.
Mochlos, 99, 104, 106, 113, 116.

Mongolia, 199.
Mongols, 195.
Moravia, 138–45, 148–50, 152, 178, 180.
Moravian gate, 138–41, 144, 145.
Moses, 55.
Mosso, 80.
Muninnikurta, 46.
Murray, Miss M., 66.
Mycenae, 113, 120.
Mycerinus, 81.
Myres, J. L., 124, 150.

NAQADA, 65, 68.
Naram-Sin, 58, 59.
Narmer or Narmerza, 69, 71, 81, 82, 171, 172.
Naruti, 58.
natron, 91.
Naxos, 99, 113, 114, 172, 175.
Near East, 13, 17, 36, 60, 96, 170.
Nebra, 70.
Nedya, 78.
Neferirikere, 76, 81,
Neforefre Shepseskere, 81.
Neith, 63.
Ne-maat-Hap, 70.
Neneter, 70, 81.
Neolithic Age, 7, 11, 14, 98, 102, 114, 122, 177.
Neterimu, 70.
Neterkere, 80.
Neuserre An or Nuserre, 81, 95.
Newberry, P. E., 64, 68.
New Guinea, 185.
nickel, 80.
Nida, 108.
Nile, 28, 29, 61, 63, 64, 68, 69, 77, 97, 99, 171.
Nile Delta, 62–4, 69, 82, 89, 94, 99, 101, 109,
    171, 172, 174.
Ningirsu, 41, 46, 50, 51.
Ninlil, 42.
Nippur, 18, 20, 39, 42, 55, 56.
Nippur tablets, 18, 20, 22.
Nish, 149.
Nishava-Morava, 149.
Nordic race, 143, 151, 190, 194, 200.
North Sea, 191.
Norway, 186, 189, 191.
No Su, 202.
Nubia, 64, 70, 73.

OBSIDIAN, 97, 103, 114, 116, 117, 126.
Old Kingdom, 61, 79, 81, 87–9, 177.
Old World, 14, 199.
olive, 63, 99.
Olt, 154.
Opis, 39.
Orchomenos, 118.
ore, 11, 13, 15.
Osiris, 62, 171, 174.
Oxford, 20, 23, 42.

PAGASATIC Gulf, 113, 124.
Palaeolithic Age, 7, 8.
Palawan, 184, 185.
Palermo stele, 26, 33, 34, 62, 63, 70.
Palestine, 77, 80, 124, 149, 152.
palette, 10.

Papua, 184, 186, 198.
Paradise, 66.
Paros, 113, 114, 116, 172, 175.
Patagonia, 191.
patesi, 44-7, 94, 178.
pectunculus, 110.
Peet, T. E., 82.
Peloponnese, 112, 118, 120, 123, 175, 180.
Peneus, 175, 178.
Peparethos, 113, 124.
Pepi I, 78, 80, 88.
Pepi II, 80.
Perabsen or Peribsen, 70, 81.
Perenmaat, 81.
Perrot, G., 87.
Perseus, 55.
Persia, 168, 189.
Persian Gulf, 13, 19, 38, 39, 54, 56, 64, 66, 171, 177.
Petrie, Sir Flinders, 30, 32, 34, 35, 89, 96.
Phaestos, 102, 108.
Pharaohs, 63, 76, 78, 83, 84.
Pharmouthi, 30.
Philippines, 184, 185.
Philippopolis, 166.
Phoenicia, 89.
Phrygia, 112, 113, 121, 123, 145.
Pič, J. L., 151.
Pindus, Mount, 113, 122.
Pisidia, 124, 149, 174.
Plynlymon type, 187.
Poebel, A., 20.
Poland, 138, 140, 143.
Polynesia, 198, 199.
Portugal, 186.
potter's wheel, 88.
pottery, 41-3, 61, 64, 88, 102, 103, 114-27, 132-6, 142-5, 151, 157-69, 174, 180.
Pruth, 167.
Psyra, 113, 124.
Ptah, 96.
Ptolemy Soter, 25.
Puenet, 77.
Pumpelly, R., 133, 137.
Punjab, 168.
Pyrenees, 191.

RE, 70, 76, 78, 178.
Rededef, 81.
Red Sea, 13, 64, 65, 77, 89, 171.
Reñeb, 70, 81.
Reneb Kakau, 69.
Reuser, 76.
Rimush, 57, 58.
Ripley, W. Z., 202.
Ro, 68.
Robson, G. C., 151.
Roman times, 15, 153, 154.
Romulus, 55.
Rosetta, 62, 65.
Rud-dedit, 76.
Rumania, 162, 167, 175-8.
Russia, 117, 139, 161, 167, 168, 189, 194.

SAHARA, 182, 183, 196, 200.
Sahure, 76, 81, 89, 90.

Sais, 63, 65, 70, 73, 82, 171.
Sakhalin, 198.
Sakkara, 61, 65, 70, 73, 76.
Samti, 81.
Sa-nekht, 72, 81.
Sardes, 104, 149.
Sargon, 54-8, 60, 177, 178.
Sayce, A. H., 57.
Scandinavia, 14.
Schliemann, H., 129, 130, 133.
Schliz, A., 143, 151, 166.
Schmidt, H., 133, 162.
Sciathos, 113, 124.
Scorpion, the, 68, 69, 171.
Scyros, 113, 124.
Seager, R. B., 102.
Seger, H., 141.
Sekhemab, Perenmaat, 70, 81.
Semang, 184.
Semerkhet, 81.
Semitic languages, 43, 44, 60, 64.
Semitic peoples, 44, 50, 189, 200.
Senedi, 81.
Senusret III, 30.
Sereth, 155, 167.
Seriphos, 113, 116.
Set, 63.
Set-folk, 70.
Sethe, K., 70.
Shamash, 44.
Shargalishari, 60.
Sharru-kin-ilubani, 54.
Sharu, 74, 81.
sheep, 126, 132, 134, 141, 156, 166, 200.
Sheikh el-Beled, 92.
Shepherd kings, 26, 202.
Shepseskaf, 76, 81.
Shirpurla, 38.
Sicily, 14, 118.
Silesia, 138, 141, 144, 145, 191, 197.
silver, 15, 104, 117.
Sinai, desert of, 13, 65, 72, 73, 77.
Sinai Mount, 65.
Sind, 168.
Sin-muballit, 20.
Sinope, 12, 13.
Siphnos, 113, 116.
Sippar, 39, 43.
Sirius, 28.
Smith, G. Elliot, 8, 10, 83, 96.
Smyrna, 149.
Snefru, 73, 74, 81, 84, 89, 177.
Somaliland, 77.
Soris, 74.
Sothis, 28, 30, 31.
Sothic cycle, 28, 30.
Spain, 14, 57.
Spercheios, 113, 126.
Spondylus gaederopus, 142, 145, 151.
Stein, Sir Aurel, 137.
stele of the vultures, 48, 49.
steppe-folk, 27, 44, 54, 62, 143, 150, 151, 169.
Stone Age, 7.
stone bowls, 36.
Stor valley, 191.
Sudan, 80.

Sudete mountains, 138, 140.
sulphur, 80.
Sumatra, 184, 185.
Sumer, 27, 38, 39, 60, 173.
Sumerian, 13, 20, 43–6, 49, 50, 54, 58, 60, 64, 66, 110, 171–8.
Suruppak, 39.
Susa, 38, 39, 43, 56, 66, 144, 168.
Sweden, 191.
swine, 126, 132, 134, 141, 156, 166.
Switzerland, 14, 156.
Syria, 44, 56, 62, 68, 69, 82, 89, 142, 152, 168.
Syros, 103, 113, 116–18.
Szabolcs County, 145.
Szechuan, 202.
Szolnok County, 145.

TAPIRO, 184.
Tardenoisian culture, 145.
Tarim, 192.
Tasmanians, 184, 196.
Taurus, 56.
Tehenu, 62, 69, 99, 101, 171, 172.
Tell Metchkin, 166.
Tell Ratcheff, 166.
tellurium, 14.
Tempe, 113, 122.
Teti, 78, 81.
Theiss, 138, 146.
Thesh, 63.
Thessaly, 112–15, 118, 121–9, 132, 133, 139, 141, 145–9, 152, 156, 160, 161, 166–9, 173–80.
Thinis, or This, 65, 69, 82.
Thisbe, gulf of, 120.
tholoi, 107, 108, 117.
Thompson, M. S., 133.
Thomson, A., 192.
Thoth, 28, 94.
Thothmes III, 30.
Thrace, 113, 124, 189.
Tibet, 192–4.
Tigris, 12, 13, 39–43, 48, 49, 54.
Timor, 184, 185.
tin, 10, 12–14, 57.
Tiryns, 113, 120.
Tiu, 63, 80, 88.
Tondja, 166.
Tordos, 15, 138, 146, 149, 153, 155, 157, 176.
Torres Straits, 185.
Transylvania, 14, 15, 70, 104, 138, 146, 153–5.
Trebizond, 12, 13.
Tripolye, 162, 164, 166, 167, 169, 178.
Trondhjem Fjord, 190.
Troy, 111, 112, 129–31

Tsangli, 123, 125, 127, 128.
Tsountas, Ch., 129.
Turin museum, 179.
Turin papyrus, 25, 26, 61.
Turkestan, 133, 137, 161, 168, 172, 178, 188, 189, 193, 194, 198, 201, 202.
turquoise, 73, 77, 137.

UAZNAR, 63, 68.
uer-khorphemtiu, 96.
uer-maa, 96.
Ukush, 53.
Umma, 38, 41, 46–50, 53, 56, 58.
Uni, 80.
Unis, 78, 81.
Unzi, 49.
Upper Sea, 56, 57.
Ur, 22–7, 38–42, 46, 55, 171–4.
Ur-Ilbaba, 52, 55.
Ur-lumma, 49, 50.
Ur-Nina, 45–7, 50.
Urukagina, 53, 54.
Urumush, 57.
Urzaged, 42.
Userkaf, 76, 81.
Ush, 46, 47.

VARDAR, 123.
Vasiliki, 102.
Vedda, 186.
Vienna, 138, 140.
Vinča, 138, 145–9, 152, 153, 157.
Volga, 161.

WACE, A. J. B., 133.
Wales, 202.
Wallachia, 154, 155, 161, 166–9.
Weidner, E. F., 20.
Weld-Blundell, C. J., 20.
Weld-Blundell prism, 22.
wheat, 134, 200.
White Wall, 65, 69.
Willendorf, 186.
Würm glaciation, 16.

XANTHOUDIDES, S., 105, 108, 111.

YEZO, 198.
Yortan, 113, 123, 124, 166, 175, 176.

ZA, 81.
Zagros mountains, 38, 39, 43.
Zer, 81.
Zoser, 70, 72, 73, 76, 81, 83, 84, 176.
Zulus, 196, 197.
Zuzu 47–9.

Printed in England at the Oxford University Press by John Johnson Printer to the University